Past-into-Present Series

SPORT

David and Pamela Kennedy

B T BATSFORD LTD London & Sydney

First published 1975

© David and Pamela Kennedy 1975

Computer composed by Eyre & Spottiswoode Ltd
at Grosvenor Press, Portsmouth

Printed by The Anchor Press Ltd, Tiptree, Essex
for the Publishers
B T Batsford Ltd, 4 Fitzhardinge Street, London W1H 0AH
23 Cross Street Brookvale NSW 2100 Australia

ISBN 0 7134 2887 2

Acknowledgment

The author and publishers would like to thank the following for their kind permission to reproduce copyright illustrations: the Radio Times Hulton Picture Library for figs 1, 2, 3, 4, 7, 8, 9, 13, 14, 16, 19, 22, 23, 25, 27, 28, 29, 30, 31, 32, 34, 35, 36, 37, 38, 39, 40, 41, 42, 43, 44, 45, 46, 47; the Trustees of the British Museum for figs 5, 6; Wayland Picture Library for figs 10, 18, 24; the Mansell Collection for figs 20, 21; Keystone Press Agency for figs 48, 49, 50, 51, 53, 54, 59, 60, 61, 63, 64; Central Press Photos for figs 52, 55; Associated Press for fig 56; Leo Dickinson for fig 57; Popperfoto for fig 62. The other pictures appearing in the book are the property of the publishers.

Contents

The Illustrations

1. Medieval Sports and Pastimes

At the time of the Roman invasion the Celts were 'a bold, active and war-like people'. They had very little time for leisure, though the simplest and probably the oldest of sports, such as running, jumping and wrestling, provided a pleasant form of training for the bitter struggles against the Roman invader.

The Romans, on the other hand, had more time for recreation, though the entertainments in their amphitheatres scarcely provided a contrast to the brutal business of military conquest. Amphitheatres in Britain at such places as Silchester and Dorchester staged gladiatorial contests, chariot races and fights between men and wild beasts. The gladiators were usually slaves, though there were some professional fighters.

Not all Roman amusements were as violent in nature. We know of ball games called *harpastum* and *paganica,* but there were no doubt others of which no record remains. We are not certain about the rules of *harpastum,* but it seems to have been a team game, in which players ran with the ball and tried to put it down behind the opposing team's baseline.

After the Roman legions had left Britain in AD 410, the country was invaded by the Saxons. Life was very precarious for these new invaders, so athletic exercises formed a major part of a Saxon nobleman's education. The aim was the development of 'hardiness, strength, and valour'.

Hunting

Hunting and hawking were favourite pastimes of noblemen in Saxon and later times. Alfred the Great 'was a most expert and active hunter, and excelled in all branches of that most noble art'. Apparently, he achieved all this before he reached the age of 12! From Saxon times the hunting rights of the common people were restricted, and after the Norman Conquest hunting became the prerogative of royalty. William I created royal forests for his hunting, the most famous one being the New Forest in Hampshire. Severe penalties against poachers were introduced, although many poor men risked punishment in order to supplement their meagre diet.

For the keen huntsman, the maintenance of horses, dogs and servants for the hunt was a costly business, but all this would be forgotten in the excitement of the chase. A day's hunting began early in the morning, when the quarry was located by the forester. Deer, wild boar, hare and rabbit were plentiful in medieval times. Blasts on the horn signalled the progress of the hunt to the horsemen and the followers on foot. Skilled horsemanship was necessary to keep up with the hounds and negotiate the fences, ditches and streams, and the trees of the forest. The exhilaration of the chase made hunting the best-loved of aristocratic sports.

1 Hunting deer on horseback and on foot. This illustration is from a fifteenth-century manuscript.

Hawking

Hunting and hawking together were considered 'the most honourable employments, and most excellent virtues'. Norman kings allowed only the highest ranks in society to keep hawks. The hawks were highly valued, and King John often accepted them as payment for revenue due to the Crown. Richard II paid £2 6s. 8d. (£2.33) for two birds — a large sum in medieval times. Masters were reluctant to part with their hawks, even in battle. Edward III took 30 falconers with him to the French wars. Of all the many species of hawks, the peregrine falcon was generally considered to be the best.

2 Hawking. Scenes from a thirteenth-century manuscript. In the bottom picture, the falconer bending down is frightening the fowls to make them rise; one hawk has just seized its prey.

Falcons were so highly esteemed partly because considerable time and effort was required for their training. They had to become accustomed to their master and to be carried 'hoodwinked' on his gloved hand; most important of all, they had to learn to return to his hand after a swoop.

When the hawking party set out, the hawks, with their hood or cap fitted over their heads, were carried on the fist, attached to their master's hand by little straps of leather called jesses. When a suitable prey flew up, the hawk's hood was removed and it would be allowed to see the bird. It was then released to swoop down on its victim and kill it with its formidable talons and beak.

3 A joust. The competitor on the right has been forcibly struck and seems on the verge of toppling from his horse.

Tournaments

Most medieval aristocratic sports were intended for participation and exercise, and did not provide much entertainment for any onlooker. However, one remarkable exception was the tournament, which was introduced into England by the Normans. The main feature of the early tournament was a mock battle or mêlée, in which heavily-armoured knights were divided into two groups, each recognizable by its distinctive shields and surcoats. The combatants charged at each other with lances and swords, in an attempt to unhorse or disarm their opponents. It was common for some of the contenders 'to be beat or thrown from their horses, trampled upon and killed upon the spot, or hurt most grievously'.

Measures were gradually introduced to make tourneying safer. There were regulations, for example, to ensure that the weapons were blunt. Soon the joust became the favourite contest of the tournament. The joust was an individual trial of strength between two knights. It took place within an enclosure, the 'lists', where barriers or 'tilts' were set up between the opponents so that the knights risked only a glancing blow from a blunted lance. The object of the contest was to strike your opponent on his helmet or chest, and either to unhorse him or else break your lance in the attempt. In the later medieval period, a points system operated — three points for unhorsing your opponent, two for a blow to his head, and one for a body-blow.

Tournaments were often banned by the authorities who considered they were too dangerous. However, they did have some military value as a battle training-ground. Their military importance was recognized by Richard I, who appointed five royal tourney fields at Salisbury, Kenilworth, Wallingford, Brackley and Blye.

As well as being a martial exercise, the tournament was also a great social occasion. The knights could display their bravery and skill-in-arms before the

4 Archery. Shooting at targets called butts.

ladies, who sat in the grandstand and selected the day's winner, and later presented the prizes. A joust was usually held in honour of a lady, and the knights would wear a token from their lady admirers — a handkerchief or a garter. The fine array presented by the ladies, the knights, their horses, the pages and the heralds all helped to create a splendid and exciting spectacle.

Jousting was forbidden for all ranks below that of esquire. Substitute amusements included tilting at the quintain, and at the ring. The quintain was a staff with an arm across the top so that it formed the shape of a T. A shield was hung on one of the arms and a bag of sand on the other. Competitors 'tilted' or charged at the shield, and tried to hit it with their lance. When the competitor hit the target shield, the arm pivoted. Unless the rider was quick, the bag of sand would swing round and knock him unceremoniously from his horse. The contemporary writer John Stow, in his *Survey of London,* tells us that: 'He that hit not the broad end of the quintain was laughed to scorn, and he that hit it full, if he rode not the faster, had a sound blow upon his neck with a bag full of sand.' Tilting or running at the ring was a similar exercise, the object being to ride at full speed, thrust the lance through a small ring, and detach it. Tilting at the quintain sometimes also took place on boats on the river, when unsuccessful contestants would receive a ducking in the water.

Archery
Another pursuit recognized for its military value and hence encouraged in medieval times was archery. The bow was the chief weapon of the common soldiers in battle, and laws were therefore passed to ensure that men practised regularly. A statute was passed in 1466, during Edward IV's reign, compelling all Englishmen to keep their own longbows and to shoot at the butts, which were set up in every town on Sundays and feast days. The butts were turfed mounds on which the target, marked with circles, was fixed.

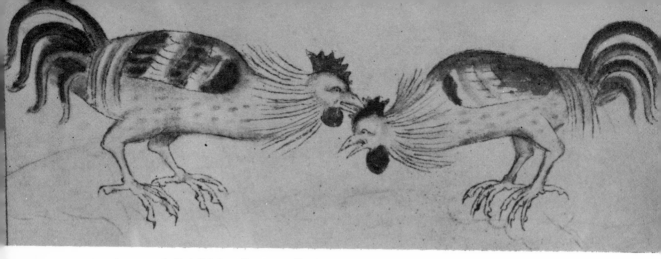

5 Cock-fighting, from a medieval manuscript. The cocks were loosed, and allowed to fight until one dropped dead.

Feast-Day Amusements

Archery practice was doubtless forgotten at the annual feast of St Bartholomew, when crowds were attracted to watch several days of sporting competition. Sword-fighting was popular, and contestants carried a buckler or small shield with which to defend themselves. These contests were so often the cause of riotous behaviour that, in 1268, a law was passed forbidding all public displays of sword-fighting. But the law was usually ignored, and sword and buckler fights could still be seen even in Tudor times, at the Cotswold Games and at local fairs.

Quarterstaff was a very ancient sport, the object of which was to wield a pole and clout your opponent, while at the same time parrying his blows.

Other feast-day amusement included the brutal sports of cock-fighting, bull- and bear-baiting, and throwing-at-cocks. A medieval writer, Fitzstephen, tells us that on Shrove Tuesday 'the school boys of the city of London bring game cocks to their masters, . . . and till dinner-time, they are permitted to amuse themselves with seeing them fight'.

Football and Hurling

Fitzstephen also depicts young men in twelfth-century London enjoying themselves in the holidays by 'leaping, shooting with the bow, wrestling, casting the stone, playing with the ball . . .' Ball games in the Middle Ages were unpopular with the authorities because they detracted from essential military pursuits like archery.

Football was prohibited in Edward III's reign. Nevertheless, there were annual Shrovetide football matches in many towns. The game was played 'in an exceedingly rough-and-ready style, with little or no reference to set rules and regulations'. The goals were set between 80 and 100 yards apart, and the ball was the blown-up bladder of an animal. The object of the game, according to one writer, was 'to get the ball into the opponent's goal by any means short of murder'. It was certainly not a game for the faint-hearted; the historian Joseph Strutt tells us: 'When the exercise becomes exceeding violent, the players kick each other's shins without the least ceremony.'

6 Wrestling. An illustration from a fourteenth-century manuscript. A man riding on the shoulders of his team-mate struggles to pull his opponent from his perch to the ground.

Hurling was another particularly rough game, which may have originated from the old Roman game of *harpastum*. In hurling the ball was carried in the hand and could be passed backwards or sideways to a team-mate. The eventual aim was to throw it beyond a fixed boundary.

Inter-village football and hurling matches were frequently held. All the village men joined in, and the pitch could stretch as far as three miles (5 km) across streams, ditches and dales. Annual Shrovetide football matches take place today in a few towns, such as Ashbourne in Derbyshire, where the match lasts about eight hours over a three-mile pitch.

Stool-Ball

There is mention in Edward I's time of a game called 'creag' which was played by his son. A curved stick or 'cryc' was used as a bat, and the game may well have been a primitive form of cricket.

The cricket of later centuries was probably influenced by games such as club-ball and stool-ball. In the former, a player hit the ball with a straight bat, and there were probably fielders to catch it. But there was no wicket. In stool-ball, however, a player tried to prevent the bowler from hitting a stool. If the batsman was successful a point was scored. The players changed places if the stool was struck, or the ball was caught by the bowler. A more complicated version of the game included several wickets, each with its own batsman. After each ball, the batsmen moved to another wicket and could be stumped as well as caught out.

11

7 Trap-ball. The boy on the left has to hit the ball as far as he can when it springs out from the trap. Notice his square wooden racket.

Trap-Ball and Tip-Cat

In the game of trap-ball, a ball would shoot out of a trap, and the batsman had to hit it as far as he could while the fielders attempted to catch it. A similar game played in the north of England was nurr-and-spell, the nurr being a wooden ball and the spell a trap. No fielders were required, since the object of the game was merely to strike the ball the greatest possible distance in a given number of strokes. (Nurr-and-spell championships have been held in Yorkshire in modern times.)

Tip-cat was a modification of these games. A cat, that is a piece of wood pointed at both ends, was struck on one 'tip', rose into the air, and was hit away by the player.

Common Games

Some medieval games are still played today, though perhaps not always in exactly the same way. Bowls and quoits are two obvious examples. Quoits used to be a popular country amusement, with two teams aiming circular iron rings or horseshoes at iron pins fixed into the ground. People in medieval times also enjoyed a form of skittles known as kayles.

Other adult amusements of medieval times have since become children's games — Leap Frog, Hoodman Blind (Blind Man's Buff), and Hot Cockles, in which a blindfolded player had to guess who had struck him. Other games included Barley Break, often called Last Couple in Hell, and Prisoner's Bars, or Base, both of which were chasing games.

12

River Sports

Adults and children alike used to enjoy games on the frozen rivers and ponds in winter. They could slide, skate on bone skates, or pull each other along on seats made from ice. Fitzstephen described the skaters: 'Sometime two runne together with Poles and hitting one the other, eyther or both doe fall, not without hurt.'

Fish were plentiful, and artificial flies were in use by the end of the medieval period. Fishing became even more popular in Tudor and Stuart times, especially after the publication of Izaak Walton's *The Compleat Angler* in 1653.

Many of the sports described in this chapter increased in popularity in Tudor and Stuart times. The tournament, however, was destined to disappear as society became less warlike, though by strange contrast, many other brutal medieval sports were taken up with still greater enthusiasm.

8 Skating was a favourite pastime in medieval times. This particular river doesn't seem very safe though — notice the man on the right who has fallen through the ice.

2. Recreations of the Tudors and Stuarts

Many sports became more organized during the Tudor and Stuart period. The favourite sports of the nobility were given an impetus by the Tudor Court. Both Henry VIII and his daughter Elizabeth were sporting enthusiasts. Among extensions to Henry's palace at Whitehall were 'divers fair tennice-courtes, bowling-alleys, and a cock-pit'.

Tennis

Tennis was usually played in a walled courtyard, although Henry constructed a special elaborate court at Hampton Court Palace. A cord and tassels served as a net, and players used short-handled rackets. The rules were complicated, and the game required great skill and stamina.

Hunting

Henry excelled in many outdoor sports, archery and hunting in particular. His daughter Elizabeth was also a keen huntress. At the age of 77, while she was visiting the residence of a nobleman, she was described as being 'excellently disposed to hunting, for every second day she is on horseback, and continues the sport long'.

Hunting remained the chief sport of the aristocracy. The forests which belonged to the Crown were stocked with stag, roe and buck. Many great households also had their own deer parks. The hunting of stag was regarded as 'the goodliest, statelyst, and most manly'. Boars were a favourite quarry but were considered dangerous game, because they relied on their strength to survive, whereas the deer used skill to escape from its pursuers. A writer says of the boar: '[it] is the only beaste which can despatche a hounde at one blow.' The numbers of both deer and boar swiftly diminished, and the boar was extinct in England by the reign of Charles I. Hunters were forced to turn to badgers, otters, foxes, rabbits and hares as prey.

Coursing

Hares and rabbits were in plentiful supply for the sport of coursing. Fast dogs such as greyhounds were used, since the dogs had to chase and outrun the victim rather than scent it out. Coursing could be held either in open country or in a paddock. A paddock was a fenced-in stretch of parkland. The prey and the dogs would run along it, in front of the spectators. The hare, or occasionally a deer, would probably be given a fair start before three or four greyhounds were released for the chase. Rules for coursing were introduced by the Duke of Norfolk, who strongly commended the hare for this sport.

9 An artist's impression of a Tudor game of tennis, a more elaborate game than our modern lawn tennis.

10 A seventeenth-century hunting scene. Notice how the hounds on the left-hand side have almost caught up with the hare.

Sports in Decline

Noblemen were still fond of hawking in Tudor times, but with the introduction of the shotgun its decline was inevitable. As the accuracy of firearms improved, game shooting became widespread. Falconry had practically died away by the end of the seventeenth century.

The invention of firearms and cannons altered the nature of warfare and made the knight in his heavy armour irrelevant. This naturally reduced the tournament's value as practice for the battlefield, though it still provided a colourful entertainment for royalty in Tudor times. The joust was gradually replaced by the less dangerous sport of tilting at the ring or quintain.

Archery was still important for defence in the early Tudor period. We hear, however, of complaints that the longbow had fallen into disuse by the time of Henry VIII. As in medieval times, attempts were made to promote archery. The Honourable Artillery Company (HAC) was founded by Henry VIII to encourage the use of 'long bowes, cross bowes and hand gunnes'. Acts were passed making archery practice compulsory, and we even hear of a bishop describing archery in one of his sermons as 'a goodly arte, a holesome kind of exercise'.

The gun eventually replaced the bow as a fighting weapon, and other sports distracted people from archery. Perhaps the compulsory element tended to make it seem a duty rather than a sport, and this may have had the effect of increasing rather than halting its decline.

11 Tudor gentlemen practise at archery while their ladies look on. By Tudor times, archery was already a sport in decline.

Fencing and Cudgel-Play

Fencing was one medieval military sport which defied this general trend, and increased its popularity during this period. Schools of sword-play had survived despite the bans of medieval kings. Henry VIII took a different attitude. He formed a company called 'The Maisters of the Noble Science of Defence'. The members gained a series of degrees as they became more proficient, the highest award being that of 'maister'. For this title, a man had to be skilled in the use of the two-handed sword, back-sword, staff, pike, rapier, dagger and bastard sword.

Village folk were enthusiastic spectators of the sword-fighting contests which were held on holy days and at fairs. They could also watch a variety of other rather violent sports and feats of dexterity — wrestling, quarterstaff and cudgelling, as well as sword-play. The object of cudgel play, for example, was to draw blood from your opponent's head by a hefty blow with your club!

12 A seventeenth-century print of village bowling. Most inns had a bowling green. Notice the spectator on the left holding his mug of ale.

Football

Football was almost as violent. One writer called it 'a devilishe pastime' from which came 'bawling, murther . . . and great effusion of blood'. Sir Thomas Elyot described it as 'nothing but beastly fury and extreme violence whereof proceedeth hurte'. A statute in the reign of Henry VIII had imposed a penalty of six days' imprisonment on anyone playing the game, but this ruling was disregarded. An edict issued in Manchester in 1608 forbade the playing of football in the town because it had led to the breaking of windows 'and other great enormyties'.

Bowls

In 1541, the government also banned the playing of bowls because they claimed that the game encouraged gambling. However, this ruling was largely

17

13 Playing at pall-mall, from a seventeenth-century print. The players had to use their mallet to hit the ball through the wire ring.

ignored, and bowls continued to be played both on open greens and in covered bowling-alleys. There was a green or alley at most great houses, inns and public gaming houses. Its association with gaming houses gave bowling an unsavoury reputation, and caused one writer to assert that there were three things thrown away besides bowls at the alleys, namely 'time, money and curses, and the last ten for one'.

Besides bowls, villagers played the skittle games of ninepins, Dutch rubbers, kayles and other variants like closh and loggats. Dutch rubbers was also called long bowling. Players attempted to bowl over nine small pins placed at the end of a narrow enclosure. The game resembles contemporary ten-pin bowling. In the game of kayles it was a stick that was thrown, rather than a ball, to knock over the pins.

Cock-Fighting and Animal-Baiting

Both noblemen and common people gambled recklessly on cock-fighting and animal-baiting contests. By Stuart times most towns had public cock-pits, and many inns used to stage contests. Henry VIII had a private cock-pit at Whitehall, and James I attended fights, known as cocking-mains, twice a week.

Game cocks were carefully chosen and reared. A good cock needed a short compact body with a round breast, and a small head, a keen eye, a stout beak and thin feet with long claws. Birds were well looked after; many were given a special diet, and any battle wounds were carefully tended.

Before a contest the birds were weighed, and pairs matched up for the fights. The tails and feathers were trimmed, and silver spurs attached to the back of the legs. With these artificial spurs the cocks could inflict great damage, and even cause death. The birds would fight on until one was either dead or else too exhausted to continue.

14 Charles II attending a horse-race meeting near Windsor Castle in 1687.

Bets continued to be laid throughout the fight. One observer noted: 'No-one who has not seen such a sight can conceive the uproar by which it is accompanied, as everybody at the same time offers and accepts bets.' Gamblers not able to pay their debts were hung above the pit in a basket as an example to others.

Those who enjoyed cock-fighting would probably also attend the bear- and bull-baiting contests. Many towns owned their own bears for baiting. One town in Cheshire is even reputed to have sold its church Bible in order to replace the town bear which had died. Animals were bred for the sport, and a Master of Bears had the job of collecting suitable dogs. As baiting time drew near, the bear or bull was fastened to a post. The dog was held by its owner in front of the chained animal until wild with fury, and then he was set on the bear or bull. Usually only one dog was released at a time.

Both the baited animal and the dogs suffered from the sport. Continual baits reduced the tethered animal's head and neck to a mass of scars and new or partly-healed wounds. Dogs were frequently wounded or killed in the attacks. Some people were disgusted by baiting; John Evelyn, a diarist, called cock-fighting and bear-baiting 'butcherly sports, or rather, barbarous cruelties'. However, most people did not share his views. Fights attracted all ranks, and Queen Elizabeth found bear-baiting quite suitable entertainment for her foreign guests.

The Puritans

Many sports, including cock-fighting and bear-baiting, were criticized by the Puritans. They also disliked the pagan associations of some festivals, and regarded dancing as 'the noble science of heathen devilrie'. Their influence in certain areas was strong by James I's reign. The King discovered that, in Lancashire, 'his subjects were debarred lawfull recreation upon Sundays after Evening Prayers ended, and upon Holy Days'. James I wanted to counteract the Puritan influence and, in 1618, he issued his Declaration of Sports which assured his subjects that they were free to follow any recreation they wanted after worship on Sundays. He recommended: 'Dancing either of men or women, Archery for men, Leaping, Vaulting, and other such blameless Recreation'.

Puritans did not object to physical exercise as such, but felt that it should serve a purpose rather than be merely pleasurable. Games were considered a waste of time, and the cause of idleness and vice. For a long time their views prevailed and, in 1642, the Long Parliament passed an act which banned most sports and pastimes.

The Restoration of Charles II in 1660 signalled the return of popular sports and pastimes. Charles himself enthusiastically played a new game called pall-mall, where a 'mall', or mallet, was used to drive a ball down an alley, usually about seven or eight hundred yards long (approximately 700 metres). Skill was needed to hit the ball through the high metal rings placed along the course, for which purpose some sort of 'lifter' would be used in place of the mall.

Horse-Racing

The Stuart Court was enthusiastic about horse-racing. Racing in Tudor times had usually consisted of private matches between two horsemen. However, racecourses were built at Chester, Newmarket and Epsom. It was to Newmarket that Charles II gave his patronage. He frequently attended meetings there, accompanied by his courtly entourage. Later, Queen Anne also proved an active patron of racing. It was during her reign that famous horses such as the Darley Arabian, the Godolphin Arabian and the Byerly Turk — ancestors of the modern thoroughbred racehorse — were imported into England.

Much heavy gambling went on at the race meetings, which no doubt explains the popularity of horse-racing in the Georgian age — a period when men seemed prepared to lay a wager not only on all types of sporting contests, but on almost any aspect of their everyday lives!

3. Georgian Sportsmen

During the Georgian era, horse-racing, boxing and cricket were established as major sports, largely through aristocratic patronage. These sports appealed to the nobility because they presented an excellent opportunity for gambling. Yet, in spite of this gambling obsession, coursing, fishing and especially hunting still remained the favourite pursuits of the wealthy landowner.

Hunting

The enclosure of land for agricultural improvement and the opening up of deer parks during the Civil War had reduced the number of wild deer. Because of this, the fox gradually came to replace the deer as quarry for the huntsmen, whereas previously foxes had been killed as mere vermin. The merits of the fox as a sporting quarry were first realized in the north of England, where packs of stag-hounds were soon replaced by packs of fox-hounds. Hares were plentiful and could be hunted by noblemen and commoners alike, but the fox provided a better day's hunting than the hare since it could travel much farther and was believed to be a more wily prey.

15 'Going out in the Morning' by Rowlandson, 1786, shows the hunt assembling for the day's sport.

16 Horse-racing at Newmarket in 1728. The race was eagerly followed by the spectators who galloped their own horses alongside the jockeys.

Horse-Racing

Towards the end of the eighteenth century, huntsmen began to run point-to-point races across rough country to test their horsemanship. Thus the sport of steeplechasing was born. It quickly became fashionable among members of the regular hunts, although it was 50 years before special steeplechasing courses were laid out.

There were already well-established courses for flat racing, and these had become social as well as sporting centres. The mecca was Newmarket where, it was said, 'you are sure to see a great many persons of the first quality, and almost all the gentlemen of the neighbourhood'. These gentlemen were very ready to lay high wagers on their favourite horses.

The classic British races all started in this period. The Oaks was first held in 1779, on the Epsom Downs racecourse in Surrey, and was instigated by the Earl of Derby, who lived near the course. The Earl also gave his name to another famous race — the Derby, of course. There is a story that the Derby was in fact very nearly called the 'Bunbury', after Derby's friend Sir Charles Bunbury. Apparently, the two men tossed a coin for the right to choose the title of the race and, as we know, Derby won. There was some consolation for Bunbury though — his horse, Diomed, won the first Derby in 1780. The great St Leger race was first run at Doncaster in 1778; its name is derived from Colonel St Leger, who provided the sweepstakes for the race.

23

Race prizes were becoming more valuable. The silver bells which had previously been presented as prizes were replaced by silver or gold bowls and plates, often inscribed with details of the winning horse. The Ascot Gold Cup was instituted in 1772, and in 1785 a race for a gold plate valued at 100 guineas. Heats were held for many of the races. One agreement drawn up for a race specified that anyone entering a horse 'for ye said plate' shall enter it 'at ye starting post of ye said heats ye day sevennight before they run'.

Jockeys in Georgian times frequently used ruthless tactics in order to win. They used to carry on running fights with their competitors whilst racing and, we are told, 'whip and kick, and attempt to unhorse each other, by entwining their legs'. The winning rider ran the risk of being attacked by those spectators who had lost money on the race. As for the judges, they were unqualified and usually incompetent. The founding of the Jockey Club was therefore an important event in the development of racing.

The Club was established in the 1750s. Originally it supervised racing at Newmarket alone, but its power and prestige grew steadily, and its authority gradually spread to all racecourses in Britain. Rules included the proper election of officials, the weighing of jockeys, and the wearing of the owner's colours for a race. A *Racing Calendar,* first published by James Weatherby in 1770, helped to standardize racing rules, very necessary since new ones were being frequently introduced. This publication became the mouthpiece of the Jockey Club. It grew so powerful that the Prince Regent himself was warned off the Newmarket course when his jockey, Sam Chifney, was suspected of 'rigging' two races.

Horse-breeding had become a serious business. Thanks mainly to the use of Arabian or Barbary sires, racehorses were now beautiful fast animals. Perhaps the most famous of all horses was Eclipse, who never lost a single race, and in all sired 334 winners.

A horse auction-room was opened by Richard Tattersall in London in 1866. It was an immediate success, and the Jockey Club soon set up their headquarters there. A room was also set aside for betting. Stakes were high, and it was customary to settle any debts the next day in the coffee house. The Georgians were heavy gamblers, and would bet on almost anything — horse-racing, prize-fighting, cock-fighting, card-playing and dicing. The Prince Regent ran up a debt of £160,000 through gambling and betting.

Cricket

Many people played cricket more for the love of gambling than of the sport. There is mention in Tudor times that 'crickett and other plaies' had taken place in Guildford, but what form this game took is not known. We hear of people being fined for playing cricket on Sunday. At Eltham in Kent, seven cricketers were fined two shillings (10p) each for this offence. The main centre for cricket was in the southern counties of Kent, Sussex and Hampshire. There was also a London Club at the Artillery Ground, Finsbury. It was there that matches between the home counties took place, as did a Kent *v* All-England match in 1711.

17. A game of cricket played on the Artillery Ground, London, in 1743. Note the tallyman notching up the score, and the use of two stumps, a curved bat and underarm bowling.

In the eighteenth century, bowlers would send the ball underhand along the ground at the batsman, who used a heavy club curved at the end to defend his wicket. The wicket comprised two stumps set wide apart with a bail on top. The batsman was not considered out if the ball passed between the stumps without dislodging the bail! One gentleman, with the comic name of 'Lumpy' Stevens, had the misfortune to bowl straight through the wicket without dislodging the bail on three occasions during a single match. It was usual for one member of the batting side to act as umpire, and he often held a stick or bat which the batsmen had to touch 'to make good their ground', that is, to complete a run. There were also one or two scorers who counted up each team's score by cutting a notch into a stick.

New techniques in the game were evolved on the Hambledon Club's pitch at Broad Halfpenny Down, in Hampshire. Here new methods of bowling and batting were tried out, and some improvements were permanently incorporated into the game. When Hambledon bowlers began to bowl length balls, instead of rolling them along the ground, the curved bat proved ineffective. Batsmen such as John Small then introduced the straight bat in order to combat this.

The width of the bat was standardized at 4¼ inches (10.8 cm). This was after 'Shock' White of Reigate had taken on to the field a bat wider than the wicket! The stumps were to be 22 inches (56 cm) high and a popping crease was cut

25

into the grass to mark out the batsmen's ground. In 1776 a third stump was added.

A code of laws for cricket had been compiled in 1744, and these were revised by a committee formed in 1774. The committee consisted of wealthy supporters of the Hambledon Club who met in a coffee house in Pall Mall. Hambledon was too remote from London for some patrons. In 1782 some London gentlemen formed their own club on the White Conduit Fields in Islington. Hambledon thus lost some of its supporters and the club, hailed by an enthusiast as the 'greatest of all elevens', was dissolved in 1791.

Thomas Lord was employed by the gentlemen of the new Islington club, and he secured from them financial backing to open a new private cricket ground on the outskirts of London, to the north of the Marylebone Road. In May 1787, the new Lord's cricket ground opened with a match between Middlesex and Essex. The White Conduit Club changed its name to the Marylebone Cricket Club. Lord's moved twice more before it was established on its present site in St John's Wood.

Other clubs came into being after the establishment of Lord's. Cricket was now played all over England at club grounds, at public schools and on village greens.

Country Sports
Cricket had not yet replaced the traditional sports played on village greens, such as tip-cat, prisoner's base and quoits. At the fairs and wakes, the men would join in wrestling contests, cudgelling, single-stick and weight-lifting, and watch animal-baiting and cock-fighting. Some amusements provided light relief — sack races, wheelbarrow races and hunting-the-pig, where contestants had to catch a pig by its greased, docked tail.

Boxing
Another feature of fairs were the boxing booths. Schools which had originally taught the nobility sword-play now began to teach boxing. James Figg kept an 'Academy' where gentlemen were instructed in 'ye use of ye small backsword and quarterstaff'. He also gave instruction in the use of fists, and staged fighting matches. After winning an official fight in 1719, he proclaimed himself England's first boxing champion.

18 (*Opposite top*) A detail from Hogarth's engraving of a cock-fight. Georgian sportsmen were willing to lay a bet on anything, however cruel. Notice the man with the sack in which the cocks are kept until their turn to fight; and the man to his left busily writing down the odds.

19 (*Opposite bottom*) Mob football, a game in Crowe Street, London, in 1721. The spectators seem just as partisan as modern football fans.

Prize-fighting at this time was a brutal affair, in which the contestants battered each other to exhaustion or unconsciousness. Boxers who were losing frequently grabbed any handy weapon and began to use it in the fight, and spectators often joined in when their champion seemed in danger of defeat.

Jack Broughton, a pupil of Figg's, attempted to ban these practices. Broughton had gained his master's title of 'Champion of England' in 1740. He set up his own amphitheatre in 1743, and this proved a great success. Broughton banned the use of weapons in fights, and he raised the stage six feet (1.8 m) above the floor to prevent the spectators from assisting their favourite. Only the fighters, the seconds, and Mr Broughton himself were allowed into the arena. Broughton also introduced gloves for sparring matches, but they were not used in public bouts, probably because they were not considered manly.

As for fighting methods, Broughton declared: 'No person is to hit his Adversary when he is down, or seize him by the ham, the breeches or any part below the waist'. Boxing technique at the time involved the use of the right arm for attack and the left arm for defence.

The introduction of rules made boxing a great attraction for all classes,

20 The fight between Broughton and Slack on 10 April 1750. Broughton was blinded in the match, and had to withdraw from boxing.

21 An eighteenth-century fencing academy, drawn by Rowlandson.

including the aristocracy. The Duke of Cumberland was a keen supporter of boxing, and was Broughton's patron for several years. He provided money for the prize fights, and was able to bet on his protégé. But Broughton was blinded and defeated in a contest with Jack Slack in 1750. The Duke lost £10,000 on the contest, and quickly withdrew his patronage. Broughton had to close down his Academy and withdraw from the sport.

Because so many contests ended in disorder and riot, boxing was officially declared illegal. However, the sport was so popular that many magistrates and constables did not dare enforce the law against prize-fights. The contests were held in secret, which may well have added to their attraction. Such fighters as Tom Johnson, George Taylor, Daniel Mendoza and Jim Belcher, continued to draw the crowds after Broughton's departure. Nevertheless, it was Jack Broughton who was called 'the father of English pugilism', and his code of rules remained until 1866, when the Queensberry Rules were drawn up.

Sea-Bathing

Perhaps one of the greatest contrasts to be found among Georgian amusements was that between the coarseness and violence of the prize fights, and the gentility and peace of the spa health resorts. Spas such as Bath had grown into fashionable resorts after the mineral water springs were declared beneficial to

29

health. When doctors recommended sea water as equally beneficial, the Georgians took to the sea, drinking it as well as bathing in it. Fishing villages grew quickly to rival the inland spas. A small fishing village called Brightelmstone was transformed by the Prince Regent into the fashionable resort of Brighton. George III had a liking for sea-bathing, especially at Weymouth, and his patronage no doubt encouraged the fashion.

Bathing was a very formal affair. Horse-drawn machines carried people down to the water where a 'dipper' would be waiting to plunge them under the waves. Men and women bathed separately, and in the nude. The Prime Minister Horace Walpole thought the craze ridiculous: 'One would think the English were ducks — they are ever waddling off to water.'

22 Bathing at Ramsgate, 1788. Notice the bathing machines in the background and the ladies in black who were employed as 'dippers', to help people to plunge under the waves.

4. Corruption in Regency Sports

The nineteenth-century aristocrat and gentleman had considerable leisure-time in which to relax after fulfilling his various responsibilities — to his country estate and the people of the local parish, and to the nation as a whole in the House of Commons or the Lords. Aristocratic sports were closely linked with country life, and among them hunting, shooting and fishing were the most popular.

Country Sports

Hunting held pride of place as the aristocratic pastime. By the nineteenth century the country had been divided up into territories belonging to particular hunts. Only a very rich man could now afford to maintain his own pack and so more and more hunts became joint financial ventures.

Shooting as a sport dates from the early nineteenth century. Partridge, pheasant, grouse and wild fowl were the main targets. It was very much a rich man's sport, since only the rich could afford the necessary parks and game-wardens. At first the shotgun was a rather dangerous weapon for its user, and there were frequent accidents with the powder and loading. Moreover, great skill — or luck — was needed to hit a bird in flight. Guns gradually became more accurate and easier to use. Joe Manston perfected the flint-lock about 1815; the copper cap came into use about 1830 and the breech-loading gun in 1853. The preservation of game was also better organized. More and more land was devoted to private parks, and professional gamekeepers carefully tended the game. Enthusiasts would spend a fortune on the sport, and most gentlemen found it socially necessary to show some interest in shooting.

There was intensified competition to obtain some of the limited number of game birds available. Rich men now expected game as a regular second course at dinner and soon an illegal poaching industry developed to supply the birds. Landowners on the other hand were fiercely determined to protect their sport, and harsh laws were passed which rigidly restricted the shooting of game. It became illegal to buy and sell game, and only squires and their eldest sons were permitted to shoot game, although this particular law was dropped in 1831. An Act of 1816 made cottagers liable to seven years' transportation to the penal colonies if they were caught trapping hares or rabbits. However, instead of discouraging the poachers, this merely made them more desperate. Poachers now worked in groups, and landowners began to use mantraps and spring-guns to maim or kill them. Frequently, though, innocent people were their victims; in 1827, the traps were forbidden. A national trade and agricultural depression meant that people were often close to starvation, and these harsh poaching laws and savage traps created great class bitterness and political unrest. Rarely have

23 Shooting snipe, 1849. Because of the expense of maintaining parks and game-wardens, shooting was very much a rich man's sport.

men shown such callousness towards other human beings just to protect their sport.

Baiting

The cruel sports of baiting and cockfighting declined during the first 30 years of the nineteenth century. A contemporary writer, Joseph Strutt, attributed this to 'a general refinement of manners and prevalence of humanity among the moderns'. In 1824 another observer, General Dyott, felt that 'the refinement in manners and habits of various classes had reached the little as well as the great'.

Attempts to ban bull-baiting narrowly failed in 1800 and 1802, and it was not until 1835 that animal baiting was finally forbidden, thanks mainly to the efforts of Richard 'Humanity' Martin. Cockfighting pits still existed in London, but the sport now found greater popularity in the mining villages of the Midlands and Tyneside. Public cock-pits were banned in 1849, though bets could still be placed on ratting and dog-fighting contests. Ratting became a craze among many working men, and by 1850 London alone had 70 rat-pits for gambling.

Prize Fighting

Prize fighting was a favourite entertainment for all classes. It was patronized by the nobility who used to lay huge wagers. In 1821, for example, £200,000 was wagered on Bill Neate in a fight against Bill Hickman. Big fights drew large crowds and nationwide interest. The sport was illegal, but was so popular that magistrates were scared to impose bans. However, crime and corruption increasingly accompanied the fights. By the 1820s the sport was in decline as fighters began to take bribes deliberately to lose a contest. Deaths in the ring occurred in 1830, 1833 and 1838, and an increasing number of fights were being won on fouls. Eventually, the sport was driven into secrecy by police action.

The contests were extremely gruelling. A round ended when an opponent was knocked or thrown over, and after a 30-second interval the injured man had only eight seconds in which to reach a square in the middle of the ring. Betting continued throughout the fight. The contestants displayed little footwork or skill; they merely stood toe-to-toe, and thumped each other with bare knuckles. One marathon contest in 1825 lasted for 276 rounds.

Declining interest in the sport was briefly checked in 1860 when Britain's champion boxer, Sayers, fought an American called Heenan. Sayers suffered a broken arm during the illegal contest, which lasted for 2 hours and 20 minutes before it was halted by the police. This marked the beginning of the end for

24 A ratting pit. Spectators are watching a champion dog kill a hundred rats in nine minutes.

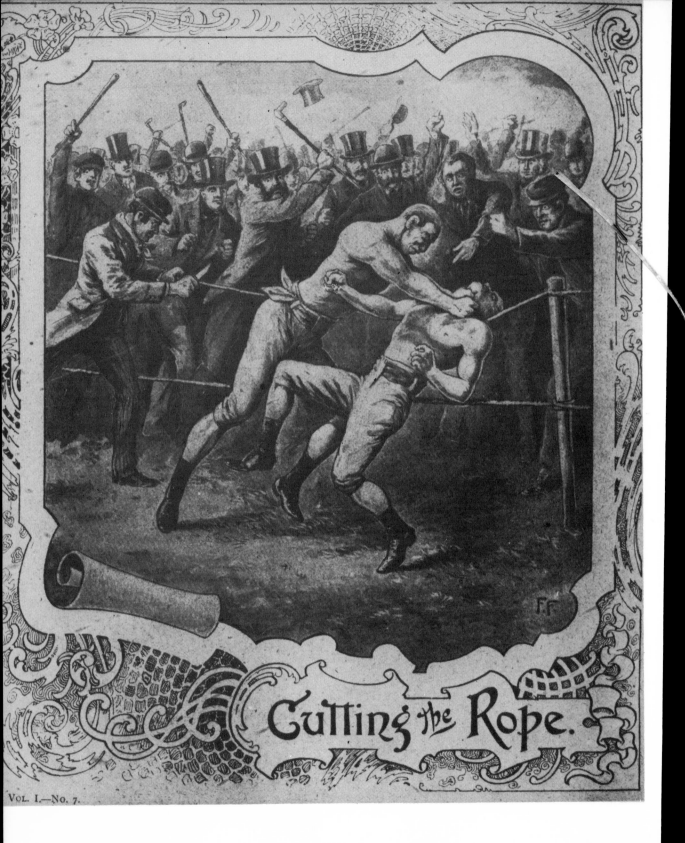

Cutting the Rope.

bare-knuckled prize fighting. Five years later, the Queensberry Rules were introduced, and the sport gradually gained a reputation for being both manly and respectable. Gloves were used and wrestling tactics banned. Official tournaments were organized, and once again the aristocracy were proud and keen to attend.

Horse-Racing

Horse-racing experienced a similar bad patch, due largely to the effects of gambling. Racehorse owners were bribed, and horses held back during the race, to ensure better odds in future events. For example, when St Giles won the Derby in 1832, nobody protested when the *New Sporting Magazine* claimed that all the other horses had been 'made safe'. Doping was rampant, jockeys and trainers bet heavily, and horses were secretly substituted or entered when over the age limit for a particular race.

The Jockey Club had begun to assume national responsibility for regulating a sport in which rules were non-existent or disregarded, horses untrained, and spectators frequently out of control. Under the guidance of Lord George Bentinck and Admiral J H Rous, the Jockey Club eliminated much corruption by insisting on punctuality in starting, the numbering of horses, more careful weighing-in and weighing-out, and the introduction of a new starting system. These reforms in the 1840s saved the reputation of the sport, which began thereafter to draw larger crowds each successive season.

Cricket

Cricket, too, suffered from gambling and corruption. At Lord's, which by 1800 had become the centre of the game, a gaggle of bookmakers could usually be seen in front of the pavilion, accepting stakes varying from 10 to 1,000 guineas. Only gentlemen could really afford to play the game, which took up so much wage-earning time, and the poorer men in the game were often susceptible to bribery. In 1817, a group of players including William Lambert, the finest player in the country, were banned from the game for 'selling' a match. However, the game's increasing popularity helped gradually to destroy the effectiveness of bribery. Previously there had been few great cricketers, and a match could depend on one man. As cricketing standards rose, the 'fixer' faced the situation of having to bribe a whole team of good players in order to obtain the result he wanted.

25 (*Opposite*) Sayers *v* Heenan Championship Fight, 1860. In the thirty-seventh round Sayers showed signs of tiring. Heenan rushed him against the ropes, forced his neck on the top strand and pressed down on his throat. The crowd, as you can see, went wild with fury and one spectator is cutting the ropes. The crowd invaded the ring, the referee disappeared and the contest continued for a further five rounds until eventually it was declared a draw.

26 A cartoon, drawn in 1806 and entitled: 'A Hero of the Turf and his Agent'. No doubt the agent is totting up what he owes the jockey for riding his horse as instructed — holding it back perhaps, to let another man win. Corruption in horse-racing was widespread, and brought the sport into bad repute.

A HERO of the TURF & his AGENT.

The amateur element in the game grew stronger as cricket began to be played at public schools and universities. Working men had also taken to cricket with great enthusiasm — by 1800 there were numerous village clubs playing informal matches. In that year a writer, Mr Pycroft, stated:

Cricket had become the common pastime of the common people in Hampshire, Surrey, Sussex, Kent and had been introduced into the adjoining counties, and though we cannot trace its continuity beyond Rutlandshire and Burley Park, certainly it had long been familiar to the men of Leicester and Nottingham, as well as Sheffield.

In the early nineteenth century batsmen dominated the game, and matches took a long time to complete. Bowlers used slow lobs or a quick under-arm, and were becoming steadily less effective. A new bowling technique was urgently needed. In 1807 John Wilkes supplied it when he used round-arm bowling and aroused a major controversy. This method was legalized in 1835, but the bowler could still be no-balled if his arm rose above his shoulder, or the ball was thrown or jerked. Bowlers continued, however, to flout the rules, and over-arm bowling was eventually permitted in 1864.

In 1846 William Clarke established an all-England team of leading profes-

36

sionals and amateur cricketers, which toured the country playing local teams of 11, 18 or 22 players for a 'guaranteed' gate. Some of the all-England players became restless — they regarded their pay of £4.30 per match meagre reward — and in 1852, John Wisden and John Lillywhite broke away to form a rival touring side — the United England XI. These sides aroused great interest in the sport and attracted crowds of thousands. Cricket began to flourish in the northern counties and was enormously popular in schools, universities and amateur clubs. The sport was on the threshold of a golden age.

Athletics

Athletics, like cricket, was able to shake off its unsavoury association with gambling and bribery to become a popular pastime among schoolboys and students. The connection with gambling had arisen in the seventeenth century when gentlemen wagered on long-distance races between their footmen. By the

27 A county cricket match: Kent *v* Sussex at Brighton in 1849. Notice the immaculate dress of the umpires, and how all the players are wearing top hats!

nineteenth century, newspapers carried daily reports of pedestrian feats, runs or long-distance walks undertaken for wagers. For example, in 1809, Captain Barclay Allardice walked 1,000 miles in 1,000 successive hours for a bet of 1,000 guineas.

Inevitably corrupt practices and rigging crept into some of these competitions, and soon gentlemen had begun to organize their own races for 'gentlemen amateurs'. From 1810 onwards, athletics meetings were held regularly at the Royal Military College, Sandhurst. In 1817 Major Mason established the Neston Guild, the world's first athletics club. Cross-country racing began at Rugby School in 1837, and eight years later, Eton started annual sprint, hurdle and steeplechase races.

Working-class men enjoyed athletic competitions at Whitsuntide festivals and rural fairs. Still popular were the traditional games in which competitors chased pigs, ran three-legged races, wrestled, or played stool-ball or nurr-and-spell. However, as the century progressed, these sports began to die out.

Rowing

Another traditional competition was a rowing event among Thames watermen. This race was instituted by Thomas Doggett in 1715 and, because of the nature of the prize, was known as Doggett's Coat and Badge. In the eighteenth century rowing had been regarded as uncouth by the gentry but by 1800 university students had begun to take up the sport. Soon afterwards, three rowing clubs were formed in London.

28 Pedestrianism in 1815. Fifty-year-old George Wilson on the ninth day of his attempt to walk 1,000 miles in 20 consecutive days. He succeeded — and won a substantial wager.

29 The Challenge Cup race at the 1840 Henley Regatta. Leander Club were the victors.

The rivers running through both Oxford and Cambridge were narrow, so bumping races were started there in 1820. Boats would set off at 100-yard intervals and if one managed to catch up and bump the boat in front, they would both withdraw and change places for the next day's race. In 1829 Oxford challenged Cambridge to an eight-oared race on the Thames. The event attracted a crowd of 20,000 and by 1856 it had become the famous annual event with which we are familiar today. The first Henley Regatta was held in 1839, when eight-oared boats competed for the silver Henley Grand Challenge Cup.

Rowing clubs sprang up all over the country. As with many other sports, the greatest enthusiasts were public schoolboys and students. It is interesting to see why sports had become so popular at school and at university, and how the aristocratic pastimes, which because of gambling had fallen into disrepute, were revived and revitalized by these young amateurs.

5. Victorian Football and Rugby

For most aristocrats in 1800, sport meant hunting and shooting, and an opportunity to gamble on various corrupt contests. No one regarded sport as a healthy outlet for physical energy, nor as being good for one's character. These new ideas about sport, which also encouraged the development of team games, and the notion of 'fair play', sportsmanship, and strict amateurism, originated almost entirely in the public schools.

Public-School Sport

Previously school sports had led to lawlessness, and most headmasters had banned games. The Headmaster of Westminster School tried to prevent rowing races against Eton, and Eton's head, Dr Keate, had stopped his school from playing cricket against Harrow. However, by the 1820s, headmasters were beginning to realize that they could turn to their own advantage the boys' natural interest in games. Boisterousness could be channelled onto the games field, instead of allowing it to disrupt class teaching.

Sport was at least a better pursuit than the usual enthusiasm for gambling and drinking. Furthermore, a headmaster of Rugby, Dr Arnold, felt that schools ought to concern themselves with the spiritual and physical development of their pupils, as well as their intellectual progress. Team games provided a happy solution. From these limited aims dawned a slow realization that sport was ideal for encouraging physical fitness. Headmasters like Cotton at Marlborough believed that team games could instill the virtues of loyalty, self-sacrifice, unselfishness and co-operation.

School Football

Football, soon the most popular team game in schools, had previously been considered a vulgar and violent sport. One aristocrat claimed that 'the amusement's too vulgar, fatiguing and rough'. Certainly mob football, with entire villages pitted against each other, was rough, and during the nineteenth century it gradually disappeared in the south of the country although it is still played on Shrove Tuesday in Atherstone in Warwickshire, Sedgefield in County Durham, and a few other places.

Most public schools developed their own brand of football, with their own rules to reduce the dangers of the game. At Rugby it remained for a long time a mob game, with at least 100 players a side. It was still mainly a chase, but players were generally expected to kick and not to handle the ball. A few players did occasionally run with the ball but the legality of this tactic was in doubt until it was finally allowed in 1841 and 1842. The laws of football at Rugby School were codified for the first time in 1846. Hacking below the knee was permitted, but players were forbidden to stand on the cross-bar to prevent a goal from being kicked!

30 A rough game of football on the playing-fields of Rugby School in 1845. A year later the rules of the game were codified for the first time.

This codification greatly encouraged the spread of Rugby football in other public schools. However, some schools resisted the influence of Rugby, and continued to play football according to their own rules. Charterhouse and Westminster schools had games which strictly prohibited the handling of the ball. When boys from different schools moved up to the universities, two rival footballing factions developed, and the need for a uniform set of rules became urgent. The first attempt at codification was made in 1848, but the rules were generally disregarded. In 1863, the representatives of six schools met at Cambridge and collectively banned the practices of hacking, tripping, and running with the ball.

London players also tried to achieve a generally agreed codification. The representatives of 11 London clubs and schools held a meeting where they approved hacking, running with the ball if a 'fair catch' was made, and tripping if the person tripped was holding the ball. However, another meeting later in the year accepted the Cambridge Rules, and soon Blackheath and other London rugby clubs withdrew to play their own game. The clubs which stayed and accepted the Cambridge Rules called their organization the Football Association.

Enthusiasm for the two games soon spread outside the schools. Sheffield, the oldest football club in the world, was formed in 1855, followed two years later by the nearby Hallam Club. It was generally middle-class men from public schools and universities who were the more skilful players, though working men's and church clubs grew rapidly in numbers and skill.

Football was then very much a dribbling game, in which a player advanced as far as possible in order to shoot at goal, and was merely followed by his colleagues who were ready to take over if he lost the ball. These dreary tactics

41

31 A comparison between the previous illustration and this painting of a game at Rugby School in 1852 seems to indicate that the game had become more orderly in the space of seven years.

were dictated by the offside rule, which penalized anyone who moved in front of his team-mate who had the ball. Fortunately for the game, forward passes were allowed in 1867, and more subtle techniques and tactics could now be used. The Football Association advertised for membership and, by 1868, 30 clubs had joined.

Rugby Football

Rugby football was frequently attacked by journalists. Comparisons were made with football: 'One is a gentleman's game played by hooligans, and the other a hooligan's game played by gentlemen.' Another person described rugby as 'a mixture of hacking, scragging, gouging and biting'. Clubs had to take their own action to prevent violence — in 1862 Blackheath banned throttling in the scrums. A central authority was badly needed since no uniform set of rules existed for the game.

In 1871, the representatives of 20 clubs and schools formed the Rugby Union. Tripping, hacking and scragging were banned, and players now had to devise new methods of stopping the man with the ball. They came up with collaring, which, as the name implies, meant grabbing your opponent round his neck and shoulders and throwing him to the ground. Only gradually did this develop into the now familiar and far more effective tackle round the legs. The ban on hacking meant that scrums now could last for a long time. Previously, hackers had waded in and scattered the scrums.

There was still no regulation about the number of players in a side, nor were umpires used. In 1874, the Rugby Union announced that clubs could appoint umpires if they wished. Not until 1888 was a proper code of penalties drawn up and referees given the power of sending players off the field. A rule of 1877 speeded up the game by insisting that a player, if tackled and still holding the ball, must immediately release it. Another improvement came two years later when players began to 'heel' the ball out of the scrum. Finally clubs began to field 15 instead of 20 players a side; this altered the whole nature of the game since there was now more room for skill than brute strength.

Rugby had become popular in Scotland and the first Scottish rugby club, the Edinburgh Academicals, had been formed in 1858. Scotland played England for the first time in 1871 when the crowd of 4,000 witnessed a Scottish victory. Since 1878, the two sides have competed annually for the Calcutta Cup. Scottish rugby has developed a more competitive organization than in England. The English game is based on 'friendlies' between clubs, whereas Scotland has a Border League and five District Unions, which have a championship each year, as do the universities.

Unlike in England and Scotland, Welsh rugby did not develop through the public schools since there were very few of them. Welsh rugby has always been a game enjoyed by all classes of people in Wales, and is in fact their major winter sport. Similar attitudes can be found in South Africa and New Zealand, and this nationwide love of the game is perhaps the main reason for the high

32 A scrum during a rugby match at the Kennington Oval in 1871.

standard of their play. The New Zealanders made their first visit to Britain in 1888. In that year the British Lions played their first matches in Australia and New Zealand. The Lions are the only team in any sport which never play in their own country.

Rugby also appealed to working men in the West Country, Wales and Lancashire. In the 1890s, a few Lancashire clubs wished to make 'broken-time' payments to their players to compensate them for any loss of wages when they were playing for their clubs. The Rugby Union refused the request, and in August 1895, 22 clubs took the dramatic step of withdrawing and forming their own Northern Union. At first they allowed only the payment of expenses to their players, but in 1898 they approved payment for services.

The two branches of the game have since followed divergent paths. The Northern Union eventually established competitive league rugby in 1907, which stimulated the need for further rule changes. League rugby has only 13 players a side, so that direct kicks and touch are forbidden, and after a tackle a player must be allowed to get up and heel the ball. These changes were introduced to make the game more open, and also more exciting for the spectator. Professional rugby clubs depended on large crowds to pay for and retain good players; by the end of the century, they were competing for spectators with the professional football clubs.

Amateur and Professional Football

Amateur football had become very popular with the urban working classes by the end of the 1860s, and thereafter very few football clubs were founded by the middle classes. Some clubs began by advertising in newspapers. On 7 March 1864, the *Leeds Mercury* stated: 'FOOTBALL — Wanted, a number of persons to form a football club for playing on Woodhouse Moor for a few days a week from 7 to 8 o'clock am.' There was an excellent response, Leeds Athletic Club was formed almost immediately, and they actually started at 6.30 am each day!

Churches provided the focal point for numerous sports clubs, since Christians regarded sport as an innocent and healthy pleasure. Southampton Football Club, whose nickname is the 'Saints', were originally attached to St Mary's Church, Southampton, and Everton, Fulham and Aston Villa also started life as church teams. Other clubs such as Arsenal, West Ham and Manchester City started in factories, while Preston North End, Sheffield Wednesday and Derby County were offshoots of cricket clubs. This extension of middle-class sports to the working class in the last quarter of the nineteenth century was due to the success of the campaign for shorter working hours and a half-day holiday.

The FA Cup was instituted in 1871 by middle-class players. Fifteen teams competed, and the Wanderers, a team of ex-public school boys, took the cup. They were to win it again five times in the next seven years. In the six years after 1879, the Old Etonians were finalists on four occasions. However, they were soon to face the working-class challenge of northern and midlands clubs. In 1878 the millworkers of Darwen held the Old Etonians to a draw in one of the earlier rounds. In 1883 public school men fell in the final to the working

33 Mob football. A cartoon by H Heath of an early nineteenth-century game of football, which was clearly little more than a brawl.

men of Blackburn Olympic, and no southern team won the final for the next 19 years.

Many changes in tactics and rules occurred during these years. Cross-bars were now used instead of tapes. Teams changed ends at half-time — previously they had only changed after the scoring of a certain number of goals. In 1871 goalkeepers were allowed to stop the ball with their hands, and the penalty kick was introduced in 1890. In the Cup Final of 1875 Lieutenant Sim headed the ball and caused great amusement! However, his novel tactic was soon taken seriously, and players also began to develop skill at passing the ball instead of attempting to dribble the length of the field.

Teams could no longer rely on just two defenders; by the 1880s they were using six. Footballers of today would laugh at the sight of a well-dressed Victorian player — he wore long knickerbockers tied at the knee, long stockings, a striped shirt, a cap, and ordinary boots with perhaps a few leather bars on the soles.

Important football games attracted large crowds, and wealthy clubs began to

45

show generosity to their players by paying their expenses and making up any losses in wages. Many talented players came from Scotland and were conveniently found weekday work in a town's factory. In 1884 Preston North End's team included only two or three locals, and the club openly admitted that players had been paid. The FA debated the question of professionalism, and in 1885 the practice was finally legalized, on condition that all professionals were registered. Players could only take part in cup ties if they had lived for two years within six miles of the club. Scotland and southern England rejected professionalism, and not until 1891 did the south have its first professional club — Arsenal.

At the start of the century, football had been played by a mob without rules. By 1900 the game was about to become the most popular spectator sport in the world.

34 An FA Cup match at Kennington Oval in 1891 between Blackburn Rovers and Notts County. Notice how the players seem to be crowding the goalmouth. The game has attracted a large and enthusiastic crowd.

6. The Emergence of Modern Sports: 1840-90

In 1800 cricket was the only properly organized team game; by the end of the century a comprehensive range of sports had developed. Enthusiastic amateurs took up the old games, gave them fresh rules, governing bodies and new techniques and tactics.

Boxing

Boxing was rescued from disrepute by new rules. The Queensberry Rules came into operation between 1865 and 1866, and introduced padded gloves, a canvas ring, and three-minute rounds. The first amateur championship was held in 1867, and the Marquis of Queensberry presented the cups for the three weights — light, middle and heavy weight. The Rules had been drawn up by a journalist, Arthur Chambers, who successfully campaigned for their adoption by professional as well as amateur fighters. There were some criticisms of the rules, particularly of the ban on in-fighting, and when the Amateur Boxing Association was founded in 1881 a new and more elaborate code of rules appeared. There were 12 founder clubs in the Association, and by 1906 the number of clubs had reached 46.

Athletics

While boxing had regained its status as a noble and aristocratic sport, the corruption and gambling associated with athletics lingered until the mid-century, when some gentlemen still felt it wise to run in amateur athletic competitions under assumed names! The first Oxford versus Cambridge athletics match took place in 1865. Clubs were being formed all over the country, and by 1867 over a hundred meetings a year were being held. However, it was essentially a sport of the gentry — the Amateur Athletic Club even barred working men. Gentlemen attempted to stop the establishment of working-class clubs in the north and midlands. Disputes were endless, the numerous rules threatened to strangle the sport, and so in 1880 27 of the larger groups organized the Amateur Athletic Association to settle arguments and act as a central body for the sport. The Association recognized the inevitable, and allowed anyone to compete provided they had never run for a money prize. Betting and money prizes were strictly outlawed.

Golf and Rowing

Golf and rowing remained even more exclusive than athletics. Golf had been played for over four centuries, but before 1850, its progress as a sport was slow. It was the national game in Scotland, and the few English clubs that had been founded were used mainly by Scotsmen. Hugh Lyon Playfair of the Royal and Ancient Golf Club of St Andrews tried hard to attract men to the game, and his efforts were helped by technical innovations such as better shaped iron-headed clubs. In 1848 'gutta percha' balls were introduced to replace the old leather ones which were stuffed with feathers. The new balls were simple to make, cheap, durable and accurate, and could carry over longer distances.

In 1857 the St Andrews course was the venue for the national golf championship, which the following year became the individual match play championship. The Royal Liverpool Club at Hoylake held an amateur championship in 1885 which later became the British Amateur Championship. Clubs and courses began to open in England, but perhaps the real breakthrough came in 1890, when the St Andrews Open was won for the first time by an English amateur, and not a Scottish professional. The idea that golf was an old man's game evaporated, and instead busy gentlemen saw it as a relaxing and yet healthy recreation.

Technical changes helped to popularize rowing as a rather more energetic upper- and middle-class sport. In 1841 Oxford were the first to use a faster 'carvel'-built boat, that is, a boat with a smooth skin instead of the former overlapping planks. Three years later came four-oared boats with outriggers — pins which held the oars eight inches (20 cm) from the side of the boat instead of on the side of the boat. Outriggers allowed narrower, faster boats to be built. Finally, sliding seats were tried in 1857. The oarsman could slide forward and then backward as he pulled on the oar, and could thus move it farther through the water.

The sport did remain exclusively a sport for 'gentlemen', and the Amateur Rowing Association ruled that no 'menial or manual' worker came within its definition of amateur. Even as late as 1920, an American sculling champion, J B Kelly, was prohibited from the competition at Henley by this rule. His social status was not high enough for such an exclusive regatta. Ironically, though, his daughter later became Princess Grace of Monaco.

Hockey

Technical improvements helped to make rowing a popular middle-class sport. With hockey, it was changes in the rules that transformed attitudes towards it. The game was a mixture of Irish hurling, Scottish shinty and English bandy, and its name probably came from the stick it was played with — a 'hooky'. In the 1830s two important rules altered the nature of the game, when players were banned from striking the ball back-handed, or tackling an opponent from behind. However, 20 years later, the game was still rough; the teams had 20 players a side and an unlimited pitch, and the rules allowed shoulder charging and shin cracking.

35 (*Opposite*) A hurdle-race at an athletics meeting in 1871.

36 The University Boat Race of 1877 which resulted in the only dead-heat on record.

More stringent regulations were introduced, and by 1886 the game had such a following that the Hockey Association was formed. Women took up the game, though their long skirts were a great hindrance and frequently hid the ball. No doubt this was occasionally a useful tactic! The All-England Women's Hockey Association was formed in 1895.

Tennis

For many years, archery and croquet had been considered the only sports suitable for a well-bred lady. Both, however, lost many of their devotees to tennis.

'Real' tennis, the indoor game, had been played since the Middle Ages. In 1874, Major Wingfield patented a new game which he called 'Sphairistike', a Greek word meaning ball-play. Players used long pear-shaped rackets to hit a small rubber ball on a grass court 30 feet (9 metres) wide, tapering to 21 feet (6.4 metres) at the 4-foot net. The game enjoyed immediate success, and in

1875 it was included by the All-England Croquet Club as a side attraction at their annual championships. Two years later, the first all-England tennis championships attracted a crowd of 200 spectators. New rules of play included the modern scoring system and a new shape of court, although the net was still rather too high for exciting play, and the service continued to be underhand.

By 1881 the game was popular throughout the country, and 1,500 spectators turned up annually for the championships. William and Earnest Renshaw proved to be the most successful players of the period. They won a number of singles and doubles championships and helped to bring more effort, determination and skill to the game. However, many people considered that tennis was merely an amusing pat-ball game for mixed company. It was bad manners to hit the ball hard at a lady. If you did so accidentally, you allowed her another shot!

37 A family game of croquet in 1865.

38 A mixed doubles' match at a tennis tournament in Eastbourne. Despite her unsuitable clothing, the lady in the foreground seems poised to make a winning smash!

Cycling

Victorian ladies continued to wear their full-length dresses when taking part in sporting activities, which proved positively dangerous when they started with the next sporting craze of cycling. This craze seemed likely for a time to replace tennis as the most popular pastime for sporting ladies. Previously cycling had been a sport for dare-devils, riding difficult machines like the 'Penny Farthing', developed in the 1860s, the 'Boneshaker' (1868) or 'Phantom' (1869). The low Rover safety cycle of 1885 replaced these high contraptions. Variations on this bicycle combined with other improvements, such as Dunlop's pneumatic tyres, the use of ball bearings, and a better braking system, caused a real cycling craze. By the early 1890s, half a million new cycles were appearing on the roads each winter.

Battersea Park was the mecca for lady cyclists. An historian, Ralph Dutton, describes the scene:

52

When the vogue began, bicycles were treated much as if they had been horses. The machine was sent in charge of a footman to Battersea Park or Regent's Park, whither the owner would drive in her carriage. Arrived at her destination she would leave her victoria and with a good deal of ceremony mount her machine and ride gracefully round and round on the broad smooth roads. The exercise over, the bicycle was handed back to the keeping of the footman and the lady would return home as she had come.

Cycling soon spread to other classes. The Cyclists' Touring Club had been founded in 1878 and by 1899 had 60,449 members.

Leisure and Holidays
Only a minority of the population participated in the sports that have been mentioned so far. The working classes had far fewer opportunities to take part. Many of them were crowded together in the new industrial towns where grass and open space had vanished. They worked a six-day week, and sport was forbidden on Sundays in deference to the Christian religion. The number of national holidays had been reduced to a mere four days a year. At the same time, the national income and wealth of the country were steadily increasing, and employers found it more difficult to resist renewed demands for longer holidays; some even realized the benefits of rest and recreation for their

39 Ladies cycling in the road, 1894.

40 An ascent of Mont Blanc. The climbers used the ladder for negotiating ice crevasses.

workers. The most significant innovation was the weekly half-holiday. One pioneer of better working conditions in the 1860s was Cadbury, who closed his Birmingham factory on Saturday afternoon; by the following decade, a 60-hour week with a half-day holiday had become the norm for millions; and by 1878 the word 'weekend' was in common usage. Working men now had the time and the energy for sport, and Mechanics' Institutes, church groups and industrial firms founded numerous sports clubs.

The Bank Holiday Act of 1871 added four extra days of holiday, and employers began to grant manual and skilled workers a week's summer holiday. But 82 per cent of the adult male population earned less than £1.50 per week. Hence many industrial workers, as well as the unemployed, the aged and the rural workers had not the money to participate in sports, even though they now had more leisure time.

Many could not even afford the extremely cheap rail excursions which followed the development of railways. The average third-class fare was between one farthing (0.1p) and three farthings a mile. At first excursionists travelled only to the outskirts of cities. As early as 1844, though, the *Railway Chronicle* was boasting that, in the first three days of Easter, hundreds of thousands were carried to 'the green fields, the smokeless heavens, and the fresh free beauties of Nature', and the railways exhibited 'a new and noble characteristic in their almost universal adaptation to the wants and recreations of millions'.

A trip to the seaside soon became the favourite outing, and families flocked to the sandy shores, sunny climate, promenade amusements, and the sea bathing. Brighton welcomed 73,000 excursionists in one week in 1859, and a year later Margate had an estimated 100,000 visitors during the year.

Swimming

Soon working people did not have to travel to the coast for a swim because many local authorities began to build public baths. The first one was opened at Liverpool in 1828. In 1846 the government passed the Baths and Wash-Houses Act for 'promoting the establishment of Baths and Wash-Houses for the Labouring Classes'. Within a few years most towns had facilities intended mainly for hygienic purposes but which led many people to learn to swim. In London, 800,000 people used the baths within a few years of the act being passed. A great impetus to swimming as a sport was provided by Captain Webb's success in 1875, when he became the first man to swim the English Channel. Swimming was now a sport for the masses, and in 1886 the Amateur Swimming Association was formed to organize and regulate activities.

Roller Skating

Roller skating had a similar mass appeal. Many attempts to manufacture a land skate had been made in the eighteenth century, but the real success came in the 1850s with the invention of the modern four-wheeled device. Improvements about 1875 produced the ball-bearing skate with metal castors, and thereafter roller skating quickly became a craze. Already by 1870 'there was scarcely a town of any importance in England that could not boast of its rink with a floor composed of cement, asphalt or wood', and the sport enjoyed a boom period in the 1880s when innumerable clubs sprang up.

Ice Skating

Enterprising businessmen also attempted to popularize ice skating. A rink was opened in London in 1842, where the 'ice' was formed from chemicals mixed with pig's lard, but this surface proved too soft for prolonged use. The first indoor rink with real ice cost £20,000 to build, and opened at Manchester in 1877. It was followed by a similar one at Southport. However, both these rinks completely failed to attract the public, and they closed a few years later. The halls were damp and musty, and skaters found them unhealthy places. By the 1890s, however, the rinks usually had good ice and pleasant conditions, and they managed to win back some customers. The Prince's Skating Club in London became an élite club for London skaters. But after a few years the public again lost interest in the sport — people quickly grew tired of merely circling round the rink, and many ice rinks only managed to stay open because of private financial support, and revenue from ice hockey matches.

Into the Twentieth Century

During the nineteenth century, working-class people had participated in very few sports. This was largely due to the lack of facilities, time and money. Between 1870 and 1890, as workers achieved reductions in working hours, so they began to take up sports. Football and cricket were the most popular, both as participatory and as spectator sports. A detailed study of Birmingham by D D Molyneux has shown that rugby football, track and field athletics, and cross-country running were popular, though football and cricket held pride of place. In the next chapter we shall examine the transformation of these two sports into professional entertainment for the masses.

41 A skating rink of real ice at Chelsea in 1878.

7. Edwardian Sport: the Golden Age?

At the beginning of the twentieth century, Britain's all-round sporting supremacy was unmatched throughout the world, and this period has often been labelled the golden age of British sport. Before the 1890s, only cricket and boxing had been taken very seriously. Thereafter, sportsmen reached high standards in all types of football, swimming, tennis, badminton, hockey and water polo, and Britain drew well ahead of her rivals. In only two sports, boxing and athletics, was Britain second best — to the United States.

Sport was regarded as a serious matter, and successful competitors became public heroes. The nation's hunger for sport led to huge crowds of spectators at important fixtures. In turn, this meant that football and cricket soon joined the ranks of boxing and horse-racing as commercialized sports, employing full-time professional players, and creating a division between the amateur and the professional.

Football

Only 4,000 people had watched the FA Cup Final in 1880, but their numbers increased rapidly — to 12,500 in 1884, and 45,000 in 1893. Lack of money and of nearby open spaces meant that many urban working men could only watch, not play, sport on their Saturday half-day. By the 1890s, many supporters carried the symbols of football fans — scarves, caps, bells, rattles and umbrellas were brought out in club colours. Newspapers reported tales of drunkenness and fighting after matches, and of vandals destroying goal-posts and wrecking property near the ground — all the complaints with which we are so familiar today. Gate receipts rocketed. In 1874 Aston Villa's receipts were 5s. 3d. (26p); for a single match in 1904 they took £14,000. Clubs were thus in a position to buy and maintain professional players.

Such financial investment necessitated regular matches. For a long time, though, fixtures were haphazard, and only cup ties aroused real interest. There were often unbalanced matches between sides of greatly varying abilities. In 1887, for example, Preston North End beat Hyde 26-0 in a cup tie. William McGregor, in association with Aston Villa and the newspaper *Athletic News*, persuaded six northern and six midland clubs to play in a league for the 1888-89 season. Generous reporting in provincial papers and special Saturday night editions helped to win public interest; very soon there was an amazing increase in the number of spectators, with League matches drawing 10,000 to 20,000 weekly. The Football League acted in conjunction with the Football Association, which it still recognizes as the supreme authority over the rules, though the League has absolute control over the League clubs.

In 1891, a representative match between the Football League and the

Football Alliance, a combination of clubs not in the League, resulted in a 1-1 draw. Soon afterwards, a second division of the League was formed, with 14 clubs, and in 1898 promotion and relegation began between the two leagues.

Players received an average of £1.50 to £2 a week, and also any transfer fees. By our standards these seem laughably low but they were regarded as huge sums by contemporaries. In 1895, Aston Villa paid £250 for an international wing-half, and in 1904, Alfred Common became the first player to be sold for a four-figure sum when Middlesbrough paid £1,000 for him. The first major ground improvement was at Stamford Bridge, where a 100,000-capacity stadium housed the fans of Chelsea Football Club. Manchester United built the even more splendid Old Trafford ground in 1910; it included a grandstand, and cover for one-sixth of the spectators — luxury indeed for those days!

By 1900 there were 300 professional clubs out of a total of 8,000 registered clubs, and the 200,000 amateur footballers by far outnumbered the professionals. There were still some public school and old boys' clubs, but the vast majority of players were working men playing for village or small town teams.

The south of England had rejected professionalism, and in 1900 Woolwich Arsenal were the only southern representatives in the Football League. Discontent came to a head in 1907, when an FA resolution allowed County Associations to admit professional clubs to membership. Gentlemen amateurs, particularly in the Surrey and Middlesex area, broke away and formed the Amateur Football Defence Federation, later renamed the Amateur Football Association. However, the effects of isolation forced them to return to the fold in 1914. The best amateur side was the Corinthians, who were able to beat the great Aston Villa in 1900, and four years later defeated the talented and successful Bury team by 10 goals to 3. League clubs favoured the tactics of man-to-man marking, and an attacking centre-half. Wing half-backs played wide to the wings, full-backs towards the centre, and inside forwards played upfield so that forwards were in a line of five.

Cricket

The length of the football season was precisely laid down — it started on 1st September and ended on the last Saturday of April. For the summer months sports fans devoted their attention to cricket, which had become much more commercialized in the last 20 years of the nineteenth century. Fans were particularly attracted by the county matches. Sussex and Nottinghamshire were strong counties, though Surrey was the most successful. Middlesex, Gloucestershire, Lancashire and Yorkshire had teams, and the game was also enthusiastically played by schools, universities and amateur clubs. Nine counties began the County Championship competition in 1873, and by the end of the century there were 15 first-class county teams.

42 (*Opposite*) An incident during the FA Challenge Cup final at Crystal Palace in 1895.

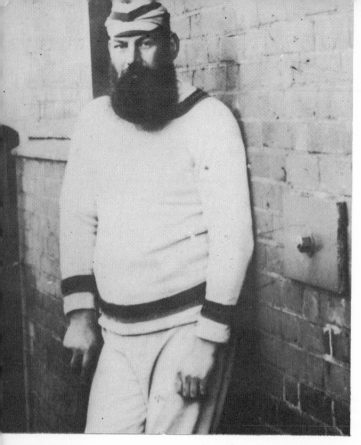

43 (*Left*) W G Grace, the greatest batsman of the period.

44 (*Below*) English cricketers during a test match in Sydney, Australia, 1898. Test matches aroused much interest in the game, which enjoyed perhaps its greatest popularity in the years leading up to the First World War.

To be really popular a sport needs to produce a hero, and cricket found one in the person of W G Grace. He played for Gloucestershire at the age of 14, and made over 1,000 runs in first-class cricket two seasons later. A wonderful eight-day spell in 1876 produced 839 runs. Altogether, he scored 126 centuries in first-class cricket, and wherever he played the crowds followed.

Test matches also aroused public interest in the game. A representative side had first toured Australia in 1861, but it was not until the 1876-77 tour that the Australians were victorious. The first official Test Match between the two countries was played in England in 1880. Three years later, England drew 2-2 in a series in Australia, and some ladies of Melbourne placed the ashes of the wickets in a small wooden urn and gave them to the English captain. They were eventually presented to the MCC, and are now kept in a showcase which they never leave, even when Australia wins the Ashes!

Many brilliant players helped England in her closely-fought test duels before the First World War, including Wilfred Rhodes, Gilbert Jessup, 'Archie' Maclaren, the young batting genius Jack Hobbs, and the great medium-paced bowler S F Barnes. During the period 1900 to 1914, pitches were very favourable to batsmen, and bowlers had to search for more effective techniques. In 1901, B J T Bosanquet delivered the 'googly' — an off-break disguised by a leg-break action. W T Greswell was the first successful swing bowler, with a right-arm inswing. In spite of these innovations, the batting and scoring rate has never been faster and higher than during the first decade of this century. The crowds at first-class matches were certainly large in number, but the real strength of the game lay in its local roots, where never before or since have there been so many cricketers.

Rugby

Village cricket broke class barriers; rugby football reinforced them. In the south, the union game was very much a middle-class affair. The split between the Rugby and Northern Unions caused divisions between the middle and working classes. The Northern Union had at first followed the rules of the Rugby Union game, but in order to attract paying customers, the rules were changed to make the game more exciting. The Challenge Cup competition began in 1896, and separate competitions for a Lancashire and a Yorkshire cup started in 1905. Separate leagues were introduced two years later.

The Rugby Union game had a lean time at the turn of the century as forward play dominated and thus slowed down the game. The number of registered clubs fell from 483 in 1893 to 244 in 1903. Recovery of rugby union as a successful sport was helped by the opening of the magnificent stadium at Twickenham in 1909 as the headquarters of the Rugby Union, and by the exciting play of the visiting New Zealanders in 1905, who proved that the game could be fast and that the backs could be used imaginatively. The crowds began to return to the rugby grounds.

45 (*Overleaf*) The Olympic Marathon of 1908 — a runner passes through the crowds of sightseers lining the London streets.

The Olympic Games

The revival of the ancient Olympic Games stimulated British athletics. The first Games were held in 1896, and the result of the last event was particularly appropriate as a Greek, Spiridon Loues, won the marathon. However, as one English competitor commented, the games were 'a bit of a lark' — the winner of the discus had never even thrown one before.

London hosted the 1908 Olympics. There were 2,647 entries from 22 countries. The Games aroused considerable interest at home — 300,000 paid to attend, and a crowd of 90,000 watched a controversial marathon in which Dorando staggered to the winning post but was disqualified because he had received help on his lap round the stadium. The 400-metres final was a farce. Two Americans and one Briton ran the final. The Briton was obstructed during the race. Officials called for a re-run but the Americans refused to race again. So one man ran alone for his gold medal!

46 A ladies' hockey game in 1910. Hockey and tennis were increasingly popular games for young women.

47 Skaters at the Princess Skating Rink in 1910, at a time when the sport was enjoying a revival.

Britain enjoyed great success in the 1908 Olympic boxing competitions, and won all five gold medals. The sport had a large number of amateurs in public schools and clubs, though professional boxing still had a poor reputation among the middle class. Major professional contests took place at the Premierland, Wonderland and the National Sporting Club, with weekly contests at London swimming baths and provincial halls. The finest boxers of the period were probably 'Peerless' Jim Driscoll and Billy Wells, who was British heavyweight champion for nine years, and Britain had two world champions in Jimmy Wilde and Ted 'Kid' Lewis.

Tennis

Tennis was still very much a rich man's game, played on private courts. The shortage of public courts and the need for expensive equipment hindered its growth for many years. The Wimbledon Championships helped to maintain interest in the game. From 1897 to 1906 the Docherty brothers dominated men's tennis, with a number of singles and doubles titles to their credit. Mrs Lambert Chambers was the outstanding woman player, and won the women's championship seven times between 1903 and 1914. However, Britain was beginning to lose her dominance to the rising tennis stars of Australia and the United States; in 1907 no English player won a Wimbledon title. The championships were abandoned for the duration of the First World War, and afterwards the United States players emerged supreme. Most competitive sports in Europe ceased during the war, but men and women emerged from their war experiences with a fresh interest in sports and recreation, and a new determination to participate in them.

8. Professionalism and Mass Entertainment

The upheavals of the First World War helped to break traditional habits of amusement; when peace came, the spread of commercialized entertainment and sport led to new patterns of recreation. The mass media helped to encourage interest in professional sport, and sports news was fed to the people through the sports sections of the newspapers, by film newsreels and later by the wireless.

Tennis

Tennis quickly benefited from sporting enthusiasm. The Wimbledon Championships of 1919 attracted great interest, and 10,000 spectators watched as a 20-year-old French girl, Suzanne Lenglen, beat Mrs Lambert Chambers, who had remained undefeated for 11 years. Not only Suzanne's tennis but her clothes astonished the crowd. Unlike the other ladies playing, she did not wear long sleeves, a suspender belt and petticoats, but instead a simple pleated skirt and stockings to the knee. This girl symbolized for many the post-war emancipation of women, and young girls began enthusiastically to take up tennis and other sports. Unfortunately tennis was still largely restricted to the middle-class members of private tennis clubs, since local authorities were very reluctant to build an adequate number of public courts.

Women's tennis play became far more vigorous and athletic. The Women's Wightman Cup competition between Britain and the United States had begun in 1923. By the 1930s British tennis was greatly improved. Dorothy Round won the women's singles title at Wimbledon in 1934 and 1937, and in 1935 Britain took both the mixed and the women's doubles titles. In 1933 Britain won the Davis Cup for the first time. Perhaps the greatest achievement was that of Fred Perry, who won the Wimbledon men's singles title three years in succession. Unfortunately the Second World War brought these triumphs to an end, for the championships were not held during the war years.

Speedway and Greyhound Racing

Tennis was essentially an amateur game and, in spite of the interest shown in the Wimbledon Championships, there was little commercialization of the sport between the wars. By way of contrast, the sports of greyhound racing and speedway, which were created during this period, were deliberately designed to be profitable mass entertainments. Both sports had the advantage that they could take place under cover and in artificial light. Dirt-track motor cycling still attracts millions of spectators annually, though it has never matched the popularity of greyhound racing since betting on speedway is prohibited.

Greyhound and whippet coursing had been a popular sport for a long time, though without any commercial organization. The first stadium for the sport was opened at Belle Vue in Manchester on 24 July 1926. Within a year crowds of 25,000 were attending the meetings, and 62 greyhound-racing companies had registered all over Britain. Five years later, greyhound racing had 18 million spectators annually, most of whom were attracted by the opportunity to gamble. The sport enjoyed a tremendous boom after the Second World War, and in 1946 the tote's turnover was £200 million. However, the sport has since declined, and the tote took only £52 million in 1962. Attendance figures have dropped from 50 million in 1949 to less than 12 million today. Yet greyhound racing still remains Britain's second largest spectator sport.

Horse-Racing

Horse-racing remains the favourite sport for gambling. In the years after the Second World War, £400 million was laid in bets annually, and the figure has now reached well over £600 million. The flat racing season lasts from late March until November. There are 58 racecourses in England and Wales, and 11,000 horses in training.

Until 1960 ready-money betting was illegal except on racecourses, and thousands of illegal bookmakers had to operate in back streets with agents furtively bringing in stake money from workmates. The Betting and Gaming Act of 1960 permitted licensed betting shops, and by 1965 there were 15,000 of them. Nowadays well over half of Britain's adult population place a bet on a sporting event at some time during the year.

Boxing

People do gamble on boxing, but most spectators are attracted by the excitement of the contests. The British Boxing Board of Control was founded in 1919, and 10 years later was given absolute power of control over professional boxing. Britain has had few world champions since the end of the First World War. The American boxers have dominated the heavyweight class, though in 1937 Tommy Farr only lost a world title fight on points to the great Joe Louis. British heavyweight champions have included Bruce Woodcock, Don Cockell, Joe Erskine, Brian London and Henry Cooper. Henry Cooper was also European champion, and in a contest against the world champion Muhammed Ali (then known as Cassius Clay), he managed to floor Ali before being forced to retire in the next round with a cut eye.

Freddie Mills was the world cruiser-weight champion from 1948 to 1950, and a year later Randolph Turpin captured the middle-weight title from Sugar Ray Robinson. Several other Britons have since won world titles, among them Terry Downes and Hogan Kid Bassey.

48 (*Opposite*) Suzanne Lenglen.

49 Randolph Turpin *v* Sugar Ray Robinson. Turpin had taken the world title from Robinson in July 1951. This photograph shows the tenth round of the return bout — Turpin is on the floor; a few seconds later the referee stopped the fight and awarded the contest to Robinson.

Many boxing halls have closed in recent years and the number of promotions has been drastically reduced. However, a new money-spinner for the sport has emerged in the form of closed-circuit television, by which championship fights can be transmitted live to the screens of cinemas all around the world. Revenue from these sources, plus huge fees from television rights, have given a few boxers million dollar purses for a single fight.

Motor Racing

Motor racing has equal cause to be grateful to television, whose coverage has won many enthusiasts for the sport. Britain had only two racing circuits until after the Second World War, one at Brooklands, opened in 1907, and the other at Donington. Brooklands was a concrete track with two long steep bankings joined by flat straights. The track was 100 feet (30 metres) wide. This had the unfortunate effect of dwarfing the cars, and destroyed that exciting impression of speed and danger with which the sport is associated. Because cars of varying power competed against each other, there had to be some form of handi-capping. At first this was achieved by adding ballast weight to the cars. Later, time handicaps were used. Grand Prix racing, however could only be seen abroad, and in Britain motor racing attracted only a few thousand dedicated car enthusiasts. Attendances at Brooklands before the Second World War averaged 5,000.

After the war, though, motor racing suddenly hit the headlines. In 1948 the

50 The Brooklands race track in 1937. Notice the steep concrete banking.

Royal Automobile Club announced the first British Grand Prix on a new track at the old Silverstone airfield in Northamptonshire, and over 100,000 spectators attended. In the same year, the Duke of Richmond and Gordon opened a circuit at Goodwood, and later came the circuit at Brand's Hatch. Since 1964 the Grand Prix has been held at Brand's Hatch and at Silverstone on alternate years. Britain soon produced world-class drivers — Mike Hawthorn beat Fangio in 1953 to win the French Grand Prix, and two years later Stirling Moss won the British event.

In 1946 the British Motor Racing Trust published details of a new grand prix car to be called the BRM (British Racing Motors). During the early 1950s it proved that it was very fast, though it usually failed to finish. Later in the decade, Colin Chapman had some success with his Coventry Climax engine, but it was Charles and John Cooper who finally hit the headlines. From a small workshop and with limited finance, they produced the car in which Jack Brabham became world champion in 1959. In the same year and the year after, they won both the constructors' and the drivers' championships. Probably the best driver of the 1960s was Jim Clark, who was twice world champion but who died in a track accident in 1968. More recently Jackie Stewart has had even greater success, winning his third world title in 1973.

51 Britain's first World Championship winner, Mike Hawthorn seen here competing at Silverstone, 1958.

52 Len Hutton receiving the congratulations of Donald Bradman at the Oval, 1938, when he created a world record Test score of 364, which remains an England record.

Excellent television coverage has stimulated racing interest — viewers can see the cars close up round the whole of the circuit, and the impression of speed and excitement is vividly conveyed. Motor manufacturers were quick to realize the advertising potential of the sport, and now drivers and racing workshops are sponsored by tyre, oil and petrol firms, and in recent years by cigarette companies.

Cricket

Sponsorship by cigarette and razor-blade firms has been an important factor in the recent revival of cricket's flagging fortunes. The game certainly had no need of help at the start of the twentieth century. However, many fine cricketers were killed in the First World War, and as a result of this Britain suffered bad defeats in test matches against Australia, with English batsmen unable to cope with the bowling of McDonald and Gregory. England had recovered by 1924, and the English players Hobbs, Sutcliffe and Maurice Tate were recognized as the world's three outstanding cricketers. Tate was considered the finest bowler in the world, and Jack Hobbs could later boast a career total of 196 centuries in first-class cricket. England finally won a test series against Australia in 1926, and then again in the 1928-29 season.

Four years later a bowling controversy embittered relations between Australian and English cricketers. Jardine, the English captain, had devised a plan to bowl to a packed leg-side field and thus limit the batsman's strokes. Unfortunately, this meant that if the bowler delivered a short-pitched ball, it would bounce up at the batsman's head or ribs, hence the nickname 'bodyline' bowling. British bowlers were accused of trying to intimidate the batsmen. England won four out of the five test matches, and in the next year the laws of the game were altered to give the umpire power to prevent deliberate intimidation.

Huge scores became the chief feature of test matches. In 1938, for example, England scored 903 for 7 wickets against Australia, and in a match against South Africa, England had to make 696 runs in the last innings in order to win! There was no time limit in tests, the pitches were 'dead', and spectators began to complain about the lack of excitement. The use of bigger stumps in 1931 made little difference.

Northern teams dominated county cricket between the wars. Yorkshire were champions 12 times, and Lancashire 5. League cricket also flourished in the northern counties. One-day Saturday matches were fought between teams of part-time players, with usually one star professional in the side. County cricket was still very class-conscious. Most of the players were professionals, but captains had to be amateurs. Professionals and amateurs used separate dressing rooms, and the annual Gentlemen v Players match still survived.

War once again interrupted professional cricket between 1939-45, and in 1945 cricket-starved fans flocked to watch the Victory Tests, and revel in the batting skills of England's new stars — Hammond, Washbrook, Compton and Edrich. Many grounds had suffered bomb damage, there was a shortage of equipment and experienced coaches, and Britain was easily defeated by

Australia and the West Indies. By 1950, our cricketing reputation had reached its lowest ebb when a visiting West Indies side won by four tests to one. Outstanding West Indian players included Worrall, Weeks and Walcott, and the bowlers Ramadhin and Valentine. Ironically, these defeats stimulated British cricket as the vitality and exuberance of the West Indian players brought new excitement to the game. The test series with Australia in 1953 maintained this revival of interest, and England won the last match of the series to take the Ashes.

The number of spectators at county cricket matches has fallen dramatically since the war. In 1949 the total annual gate was 2,126,000. By 1955 the figure was down to 1,641,000, and the downward trend has since continued. Cricket authorities became so worried that they set up a special committee to discover why county cricket had lost its appeal. The committee blamed the defensive bowling that had developed since the war, as bowlers concentrated their fielders on the leg side and bowled to the leg stump. Better fielding and crumbling pitches had also made life difficult for the batsmen. The result was that the average run rate had dropped to half that of the inter-war years. To improve matters, the special committee recommended a limit on the number of legside fieldsmen, and suggested shortened boundaries and faster pitches.

These changes, however, had little effect, and in fact county cricket has only been kept alive by revenue from test matches, supporters club football pools, and the recent one-day competitions. Since 1963 the counties have competed in a single innings competition for the Gillette Cricket Cup, and in 1969 the John Player Sunday League began. A third competition to be added recently is the Benson and Hedges Cup. Many professionals now have to play for seven days a week, and it seems unlikely that three-day county championship matches will continue in their present form for much longer.

Football

Professional footballers are faced with similar extra demands because of the European cup competitions, and the extension of the football season forward into May and back into August. In the earlier part of this century Britain had remained aloof from European football, and had left the Federation of International Football Associations (FIFA) because of arguments over 'broken-time' payments for amateurs. The British regarded themselves as masters of the game, and concentrated their attention on domestic League and Cup fixtures. In 1920 a third Division began, with 22 clubs from the Southern League, and a year later a northern section.

Rule changes affected football tactics. The offside law was amended in 1925 — there now had to be fewer than two men instead of three between the attacker and the goal for the man to be declared offside. The immediate effect of this was a greater number of goals, and the innovation of the 'stopper' centre half. Arsenal, under the managership of Herbert Chapman, were the most successful team at devising new tactics. They had forwards who could out-manoeuvre the defences held back to check them. Inside forwards were kept to the rear as link men between defence and attack. The aim was to be as direct as possible — to reach your opponents' penalty area with a minimum of moves. Arsenal achieved magnificent results in the 1930s, winning the League championship four times and the Cup twice. Though they dominated the football scene, there were other fine teams. Huddersfield Town had won the League three years in succession between 1924 and 1926, and Sheffield Wednesday won it twice in 1929 and 1930. Manchester United enjoyed FA cup success, and Everton possessed a brilliant centre-forward, Dixie Dean, who shattered all goal-scoring records.

League football did not cease during the Second World War — it was retained to boost the nation's morale. The League was divided into regular competitions, and spectators frequently found the following notice in their programme:

> In the event of an Air Raid Warning being received, the police will instruct the referee to stop the game, and the players will leave the field. Spectators must take shelter, and remain under cover until the All Clear has been given.

After the war British football cast aside its insular attitude, and began to take part in European and world competitions. Soon after the war, Moscow Dynamo became the first Russian team to visit England. Britain rejoined FIFA in 1947, and in that same year Walter Winterbottom was appointed as England's team manager. His first entry into international football was a disaster when, in 1950, England was beaten 1-0 in the World Cup, by the United States! Perhaps the turning-point for British football came in 1953 when Hungary won 6-3 in a decisive British defeat. The sheer skill and tactical brilliance of the Hungarians made people at home realize that British footballers no longer reigned supreme, and that they must look outwards, revise their style of play, and learn from continental sides. The modern footballer could not be just a worker; and he had to be an athlete and an artist as well, a man who was fast and intelligent, and interchangeable on the field.

The successful Wolves' side of the 1950s, managed by Stan Cullis, developed a distinctive style of directness and speed. And the motto of Spurs was: 'Make it simple, make it quick.' Their style became known as 'push and run' since their manager rejected the idea that players should take on and beat their man, but instead thought that they should use quick passing in order to advance. Spurs' new manager, Bill Nicholson, adopted this style in the early 1960s, and soon had made them the most successful side in the British League; in 1963 they won the European Cup Winners' Cup. Manchester United had been the first English side to enter the European Cup in 1956, and it was appropriate

53 (*Opposite*) England players chair their captain Bobby Moore after winning the World Cup final at Wembley in 1966.

that they should be the first English team to win the competition when they defeated Benfica in 1968. There was a truly emotional moment at the end of the match as the brilliant United player Bobby Charlton and the team manager Matt Busby greeted each other. Both had striven for years to win this Cup, and had survived a terrible air crash a few years earlier which had wiped out most of their team.

England has also tasted success in the World Cup. Alf Ramsey was appointed team manager in 1963 and England won the World Cup in 1966. The exciting final at Wembley went to extra time before West Germany were eventually beaten 3-1. This success revived flagging interest in the game. In the 1948-49 season the total League attendance figure was 40 million. This had dropped to 33½ million in 1958-59, to 28 million in 1960-61, though it rose to 29 million in the 1966-67 season.

There is no doubt that British clubs have been very successful recently in European competitions. Celtic have won the European Cup, and the UEFA cup final of 1972 was an all-British affair won by Spurs. Glasgow Rangers took the European Cup Winners' Cup in the same year. Perhaps, though, the game will never again achieve its position of pre-eminence as a spectator sport. Many people prefer to use Saturdays for family outings in the car. Also there is a vast range of different sports now readily available to young people, and increasingly people are turning to the non-competitive sports.

9. Sport for All

Young people in the 1920s reacted against the misery and hardship of the war years by taking enthusiastically to outdoor sports. Thousands poured from the towns at weekends to cycle and to camp, to hike and to swim in the countryside. The Boy Scout and Girl Guide movements flourished, and the Youth Hostels Association was founded. The membership of the Camping Club, Cyclists' Touring Club and the Ramblers' Association increased greatly in the 1930s as people responded to the new gospel of fresh air and exercise.

The Government and Sports

British governments were slow to respond to this enthusiasm for physical fitness and sport. Did sport contain its own justification, or should it be supported in order to produce a healthy industrial working-force or a potential army? The government resolved not to be directly concerned with the organization or promotion of sport, but to encourage it by giving financial aid to national, local and voluntary sporting organizations. However, far too little money was available to meet the problems. In 1929 the London County Council received applications from 1,000 clubs who wanted cricket pitches; they could provide only 350. 85 hockey clubs had somehow to share 26 pitches. 65,000 London tennis players had only 815 courts at their disposal. Playing fields were almost non-existent, and most children were forced to play in the streets.

Both local and national government response to this crisis was feeble. The National Playing Fields Association did start to provide areas for young people to play in the 1930s. In 1932 the LCC allowed games in London parks on Sundays, and in 1934 permitted the playing of football and cricket matches in the parks. The Physical Training and Recreation Act of 1937 voted £2 million for sport, and extended the powers of the government and local authorities to make grants to voluntary bodies, such as the Central Council of Physical Recreation. The government also set up the National Fitness Council. Some local authorities and industrial firms showed an imaginative interest in sport, and new swimming pools and other facilities were opened. But all this was done on a very piecemeal basis.

54 (*Overleaf*) Scouts from all over the world gather at Sutton Coldfield for the opening of the World Scout Jubilee Jamboree, 1957. Outdoor activities such as scouting appeal to youngsters everywhere.

The start of the Second World War, however, soon changed government attitudes towards sport. A campaign of 'fitness for service' began, and both men and women, whether in the army or not, were encouraged to take rigorous exercise. More importantly, the war forced the government to consider methods of improving the physical fitness of future generations. The Education Act of 1944 made the provision of facilities for sport obligatory on all local education authorities. For the first time, sport, as distinct from physical training, became a compulsory part of the state schools' curriculum.

The newly formed Central Council of Physical Recreation began very useful coaching work in many sports, but after the war there were growing complaints that the government still gave virtually no financial aid to sport. Unfortunately the governing bodies of sporting associations were reluctant to press too vigorously for help because they were afraid of government interference. The government responded by setting up the Wolfenden Committee, and in 1960 it reported on 'Sport and the Community'. Its most important conclusion was that 'there is a positive "play" element in the life of young people, which can be neglected only to the disadvantage of both the individual and society'.

55 Edmund Hillary and Sherpa Tensing arrive back in London after the first successful ascent of Everest in May 1953.

56 Anne Packer winning the women's 800 metres gold medal at the Tokyo Olympics, 1964.

In 1965 the Labour government appointed the first Minister of Sport, and set up the Sports Council to advise the government on the development of amateur sports and physical recreation. Regional sports councils bring together representatives of local authorities, voluntary sports organizations and the government departments concerned. The new Sports Councils, set up in 1971, are no longer simply advisory. They are responsible for giving grants to encourage the development of sport, though local authorities are still the greatest providers.

At least a quarter of the present adult population is interested in playing a sport, or is a regular spectator. In recent years, the government at Westminster has certainly accepted more responsibility for financial aid to sport. However, the following table reveals that our European neighbours are prepared to spend even more:

Amount spent on sport per head of population

Great Britain	47p
West Germany	£1.27
France	£1.35
Holland	£1.78

(*1968 figures issued by the Sports Council*)

The government collects over £30 million annually from its taxes on sport, and this money could easily be ploughed back into sport. In all except three European countries, football pools are controlled by the state, which then hives off a proportion of the profits and uses it to encourage other sporting activities.

The British people are perhaps too cautious in worrying about the morality of the state helping to finance our sporting representation on the international field. Generally at the moment, British participation in sports internationals is financed by the governing body concerned. For the Olympic and Commonwealth Games, finance comes from voluntary subscriptions. For the last Olympic Games (1972), we had the supreme irony of the principal sponsorship coming from a cigarette firm, whose packets carried government warnings about the possible dangers of smoking to health!

The Sports Council is currently conducting an energetic 'Sport for All' campaign, aimed at stirring local authorities and others into providing amenities at the rate of £35 million a year for ten years. People have an increasing amount of leisure time and money to spend on sport, and it is vital that proper provision for sports can match demand, otherwise we shall all be forced into the role of mere spectators and gamblers.

57 (*Opposite*) Mountaineering and climbing are increasingly popular sports. Here a climber uses ropes to negotiate a tricky overhang.

58 (*Below*) Caving, another popular pastime.

59 The excitement of canoeing.

Participation in Sport

There are many reasons for the upsurge of interest in sport. People nowadays have more free time, and more money to spend. Trade unions have fought hard to win longer holidays for their members. The Holidays with Pay Act of 1938 established the principle that every worker was entitled to at least one week's annual holiday with pay, and by the end of the 1960s two weeks in addition to public holidays had become the norm. The weekend was extended by the adoption of a five-day working week, which spread rapidly after 1945. The average hours in a working week were reduced from 50 in 1939, to 44 in 1961, and today the usual is about 40 hours. This reduction has not had dramatic effects because many workers prefer to work a few hours overtime in order to increase their pay. Labour-saving devices in the home and smaller families have freed married couples from time-consuming household chores.

Restrictions on Sunday sport have been lifted in recent years. The Crathorne Committee's Report of 1964 on the law of Sunday observance recommended that virtually all sports should be permitted, except matches involving the payment of players. Since then, even this ruling has been relaxed to allow, for example, the John Player League cricket competition.

Non-Competitive Sports

Finally, the motor car has opened up a new range of sports to ordinary people. The number of privately-owned cars has risen from 200,000 in 1920 to 2 million in 1939, and nearly 11 million by 1965. At weekends many people head for the countryside in pursuit of newly popular sports such as canoeing, sailing, climbing and caving. This back-to-nature trend is partly a reaction against urban living, but it also reflects a search by young people for adventure and danger. Since the war, team games have undoubtedly lost in popularity compared with sports where the competitive element is less important than the exercise and development of particular skills.

There are now over 200 mountaineering clubs in Britain, and both climbing and hill-walking are extremely popular among young people. Skiing is being developed in Scotland, and facilities at Aviemore in the Cairngorms are now good enough to attract thousands of enthusiasts on winter weekends.

There has been a 1,000 per cent increase in small boat ownership over the last ten years. The number of people sailing dinghies at weekends rose from an

60 The ski lift at Glenshee in Scotland.

estimated 13,000 in 1950 to a quarter of a million in 1964. Now, about 3 million people go sailing at some time during the year, and the Royal Yachting Association has 1,550 affiliated clubs.

Angling is immensely popular, with an estimated 4 million devotees. Coarse fishing is the most widely practised, though many enjoy sea and deep-sea fishing. Of the other two 'classic' sports, shooting is still largely the preserve of the wealthy, but hunting has been taken up by a far greater number of people. The fox is the chief quarry, though there is some stag hunting, and the hare is hunted on foot with beagles.

Judo, fencing, badminton and squash are examples of competitive sports which are becoming very popular. Judo received a great boost when Britain secured a silver and a bronze medal in the 1972 Olympic Games. Facilities for fencing and squash have previously been severely limited, but now new sports centres invariably include them in their provision, and by 1971 there were nearly 700 fencing clubs.

61 Brian Jacks of Britain in action against Seung Lip Ho of Korea, in the Judo middleweight event, Munich 1972.

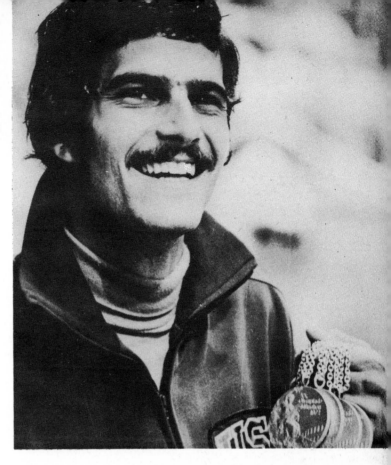

62 Mark Spitz holding some of the seven gold medals he won for swimming at the Munich Olympics, 1972. But Spitz aroused a storm of controversy when he was seen openly advertising a particular type of training shoe. This contravened the Olympic rules, which say that only amateurs, not professionals, may compete.

By contrast, some traditionally popular competitive sports have lost ground in recent years. Rugby union certainly has, though amateur football still flourishes with nearly a million amateur players, and 32,000 clubs affiliated to regional associations.

In spite of all this sporting activity there has been a general decline of physical fitness in Britain, due largely to the decrease in casual physical exercise — climbing stairs, walking to work — and to an increase in the consumption of food and drink. Sport is now more important than ever for maintaining the nation's health, although ironically many of the popular new sports require a minimum of physical exercise. Water-skiing and go-kart racing are striking examples of this trend. Skiing, ten-pin bowling and golf rely on mechanical aids, while sailing and angling generally make little physical demand. It cannot be mere coincidence that these sports have increased their following faster than most.

Amateur or Professional?

Athletics and tennis are certainly very strenuous, yet they have maintained their popularity. This is probably because they are exciting for the spectators, and hence receive plenty of newspaper and television coverage; this in turn encourages youngsters to take up the sport. Both these sports were troubled during the 1960s with the problems of 'shamateurism', that is, the illegal payment of top amateurs. By 1968 all the leading tennis players had turned

89

63 A demonstration against apartheid in sport. This march took place in 1969 at Twickenham, before the start of the England *v* South Africa rugby international.

professional. In the same year, the British Lawn Tennis Association announced that Wimbledon would be open to professionals. As a result Britain was suspended from the International Lawn Tennis Federation. Today, however, all major tournaments are open to all, and there is now a possibility that the top players may ignore the European tournaments in order to play in the very profitable American league tennis.

All distinctions between the amateur and the professional player were dropped from cricket in 1963, and from football in 1974. Professionalism, however, is still very much a live issue for the Olympic Games committee. In 1972 one of the world's top skiers, Karl Schranz, was expelled from the Winter Olympics for blatant commercialism. Many businesses spend a great deal of money on athletes in order to secure good publicity and advertise their products. Sponsoring has also given a significant impetus to sports in Britain.

Seven sports — motor racing, soccer, golf, tennis, horse racing, cricket and show-jumping — received over £300,000 each in 1972, and some of them well over this figure. It is an accepted fact that many governments around the world give considerable support to their athletes, who are in practice, if not in name, full-time professionals. Sport has become one more battle-ground in the conflict of political systems.

Politics in Sport

Perhaps the first evidence of this trend was at the 1936 Olympic Games, where Hitler looked for proof of his theory of Aryan superiority. By 1956 Russia was spending an estimated £30 million to achieve Olympic success. Two years later, the official Soviet newspaper, *Pravda* pointed out:

> A successful trip by the sportsmen of the USSR or the People's Democratic countries is an excellent vehicle of propaganda in capitalist countries. The success of our sportsmen abroad helps in the work of our foreign diplomatic missions and our trade delegations.

64 Photo taken during the raid on the Munich Olympic Village by Arab terrorists, 1972. The growing incidence of such attacks is causing fear, lest sport should increasingly be used as a political weapon.

Politics have increasingly intruded on sport. Demonstrations disrupted the South African rugby tour of Britain in 1969, and the South African cricket tour was cancelled after public pressure in 1970. South Africa has also been banned from Davis Cup tennis and Olympic competition because her apartheid policies prevent her from sending a truly representative team. International matches in Northern Ireland have recently been cancelled for fear of IRA terrorism. American athletes gave publicity to the Black Power movement at the 1968 Olympics. But perhaps the most dramatic and tragic incident of political interference was the killing of Israeli athletes at the 1972 Munich Olympic Games by members of the Palestine Liberation movement.

A world-wide audience of 500 million watched the Munich Olympics. Such an opportunity for political propaganda inevitably proved irresistible. In the future, we must expect international sport to become even more fiercely nationalistic and riddled with political or commercial overtones. We must hope, though, that the professionals, in striving to win, will not kill enjoyment of the sport, and will still be capable of inspiring young people to take up sport for relaxation, health and pleasure.

Further Reading

General Books
J Arlott and A Daley, *Pageantry of Sport* (Elek, 1968)
Central Council of Physical Recreation, *Sport and the Community* (Report of the Wolfenden Committee, 1960)
Central Office of Information, *Sport in Britain* (HMSO, 1972)
C Hole *English Sports and Pastimes* (Batsford, 1949)
P C McIntosh, *Games and Sports* (Information Books: How Things Developed, Ward Lock, 1962)
P C McIntosh, *Sport in Society* (C A Watts, 1964)
P Moss, *Sports and Pastimes through the Ages* (Harrap, 1962)
Oxford Junior Encylopedia, Vol 9, *Recreations* (OUP)
J A R Pimlott, *Recreations* (Studio Vista, 1961)
N Wymer, *Sport in England* (Harrap, 1949)

Boxing
N Fleischer and S Andre, *Pictorial History of Boxing* (Spring Books, 1966)

Cricket
H S Altham and E W Swanton, *A History of Cricket* (2 vols) (Allen and Unwin, 1968)
B J W Hill, *Cricket* (Blackwell, 1960)
Brian Johnston, *All about Cricket* (W H Allen, 1972)

Golf
N Gibson, *A Pictorial History of Golf* (Yoseloff, 1968)

Ice-Skating
Nigel Brown, *Ice-Skating: a History* (Nicholas Kaye, 1959)

Motor Racing
R Garrett, *The Motor Racing Story* (Stanley Paul, 1969)

Mountaineering
S Styles, *On Top of the World* (Hamish Hamilton, 1967)

Rugby
T Hughes, *Tom Brown's Schooldays* (Macmillan, 1967)
O L Owen, *History of the Rugby Football Union* (Playfair Books, 1955)

Seaside
A N Hern, *The English Seaside* (Cresset Press, 1967)

Soccer
T Delaney *A Century of Soccer* (Official Football Association Publication; Heinemann, 1963)
D Signy *A Pictorial History of Soccer* (Hamlyn, 1968)
P M Young *History of British Football* (Stanley Paul, 1968)

Tennis
Lord Aberdere, *The Story of Tennis* (Stanley Paul, 1959)

Tournament
Stephen Jeffreys, *Tourney and Joust* (Wayland, 1973)
R J Mitchell, *The Medieval Tournament* (Longman)

INDEX

The numbers in **bold** refer to the figure numbers of the illustrations.